COOK NOW
EAT LATER

COOK NOW EAT LATER

Mary Berry

Photographs by Peter Cassidy

headline

Recent books by Mary Berry
The New Cook
Mary Berry Cooks Puddings and Desserts
Mary Berry Cooks Cakes
Mary Berry at Home
The Complete Cookbook
The Ultimate Cake Book
Quick and Easy Cake Book
Mary Berry's New Aga Cookbook

First published in 2002
by HEADLINE BOOK PUBLISHING

First published in softback in 2006
by HEADLINE BOOK PUBLISHING

3

Cataloguing in Publication Data is available from the British Library

ISBN 978 0 7553 1016 6

Photographs by Peter Cassidy
Edited by Susan Fleming
Designed by Isobel Gillan
Typeset by Letterpart Limited, Reigate, Surrey
Colour reproduction by Spectrum Colour
Printed and bound by Rotolito Lombarda, Italy

Headline's policy is to use papers that are natural, renewable and recyclable products
and made from wood grown in sustainable forests. The logging and manufacturing processes
are expected to conform to the environmental regulations of the country of origin.

HEADLINE BOOK PUBLISHING
A division of Hodder Headline
338 Euston Road
London NW1 3BH

www.headline.co.uk
www.hodderheadline.com

CONTENTS

Lucy Young and Mary Berry

A DEDICATION
AND SOME THANK YOUS

The book is dedicated to Lucy Young who has worked with me now for twelve years. I cannot imagine there being a day, or my doing a book, without her by my side. She runs my working life, is practical, full of inspirational ideas and what's more, for a trained cook, is a dab hand with computers and disks (something I know nothing about and have no wish to either)! This is the first book we've done by e-mail: for me it usually starts with a large foolscap pad and an awful lot of scrawl. Lucy is definitely a cherished member of the family, and we have such fun working together. She is not my daughter, although everyone thinks she is, but I treat her like my daughter and she treats me like her second mum! Lucy and the rest of my family are trying hard to make me slow down and say no to more cooking commitments and charity demonstrations, and to do fewer Aga Workshop days. But for me it is very difficult to slow down when I just love what I do, and I have the greatest team to help me.

This is the seventh book that Fiona Oyston has helped us with, testing recipes using her meticulous cooking skills. She spent many years as assistant cookery editor with *Good Housekeeping* which, to my mind, has the best cookery department, together with BBC *Good Food Magazine*. I would also like to thank Lucinda Kaizik, who has helped Lucy for nearly two years. She has helped test the recipes in the Aga here at Watercroft, and more often than not goes back home and cooks them in her mum's Aga for supper again!

My cooking certainly has changed over the years. I have to thank our young for keeping me very much in touch: Tom and his darling wife Sarah, and Annabel and Dan. When we've had a day's testing they often take the food home and follow the reheat instructions (as in this book) for supper and tell me honestly how it worked. Annabel, a brilliant cook herself, has contributed too with ideas from her gadding about, many of them vegetarian. And of course I mustn't forget my lovely husband Paul. When I write a book he obviously eats very well for about eighteen months, although anything more ambitious than shepherd's pie or roast beef he tends to call 'mucked-about food'.

I count myself very lucky running my Aga Workshop Cookery School. I am in constant contact with 'punters', many of whom have become great friends over the years. From them I get hand-written recipes on backs of envelopes, and variations on some of my old recipes they have tried, and much encouragement.

And finally I would like to thank all the team at Headline, particularly Heather Holden-Brown for asking me to write the book. That call at 6.15 one Friday evening some eighteen months ago seems an age away now. A huge thank you to the wonderful Celia Kent, our editor, who has masterminded this book from the beginning. It's the second book we have worked together on and again it's been an absolute pleasure. Thanks are due also to the lovely Susan Fleming, who ensured every detail in this book is clear and precise, to Felicity Bryan, my book agent for more years than I can remember, and finally to you, all the readers who have encouraged me over the years with letters of support and photos of your triumphs. I do so hope you enjoy this book, and that it makes your life in the kitchen easier and more hassle free.

INTRODUCTION

This book is all about being organised. It's about preparing and cooking ahead, whether you are feeding the family casually in the kitchen or friends more formally in the dining room. We all love entertaining, but sometimes the reality of the many separate parts involved in a meal can seem daunting. How long will the pudding take to set? When can I prepare the vegetables? Will the potatoes be ready at the same time as the meat? Will the whole house smell of fish when I sear the sea bass skin? When can I talk to my friends if I'm stuck in the kitchen? Panic can set in, but that's where I will come to your rescue.

In a book such as this, where the concept is 'cook now, eat later', it would be easy to give you recipes that could all be cooked completely in advance, and that merely needed reheating. Easy, yes, but a bit boring. What I have done is gather together my very latest, up-to-the-minute recipes, many of which, I will happily admit, need some last-minute attention. But various stages of them can be prepared and/or cooked in advance, which means that on the day itself, you will have much less to do, and will not feel too much under immediate pressure. The recipes themselves are divided into easy-to-follow numbered steps, and that's essentially what I want to do here: help you to be one step ahead of the game.

Being organised so far as food and entertaining are concerned is not just to do with the actual cooking. For instance, if you order the fish or meat you want well in advance from fishmonger, butcher or supermarket, that's one aspect of the meal taken care of. We all think freshly prepared is best, but many vegetables can be peeled, trimmed and cut at least the day before, which means one less chore on the day. And don't ever be ashamed of cutting corners to enable you to be organised and ahead. Buy ready-prepared vegetables or salad leaves in packets if you think you won't have time: they're more expensive, but your peace of mind might be more important than cost. Even counting out the napkins, and checking on candles and cutlery a couple of days in advance, puts you a step or so ahead.

But the majority of the information here does actually concern some degree of cooking, and when you are doing this in advance, there are certain stages which must be followed. The refrigerator is intimately involved in this, and the 'rules' concerning cooling and chilling are particularly important. Make sure your fridge is working properly. The ideal temperature for the short-term storage of perishable foods is just above freezing point. Individual makes of fridges vary, but the temperature range should be between 1° and 7°C (34°–44°F).

Preparing and Cooking Ahead

I won't detail every single way in which you can prepare and cook ahead, but just give you a few general ideas.

Firstly preparation, which does not require cooking. Many non-cooked cold starters and desserts can be completely prepared ahead and stored in the fridge, to set and/or chill. Meats, fish and vegetables can be marinated overnight in the fridge, ready for cooking the next day. Many vegetables can be prepared in advance, and kept raw in the fridge. Savoury butters – handy for so many uses – last well in the fridge, and some uncooked stuffings can be assembled with meats or fish, and carefully chilled until it's time to cook. (Always buy the very finest quality of freshest fish and meat.) Raw pastry, bought or home-made, positively benefits from being kept in the fridge, after rolling and cutting into the desired shapes.

Everything must be carefully covered, to prevent smells permeating where they shouldn't, or surfaces drying. Clingfilm and foil are invaluable tools for those who want to get ahead! Some foods need to breathe when stored, like cheese, which is best wrapped in greaseproof or wax paper.

Cooking ahead perhaps lies at the heart of the book. Many dishes require part-cooking a day or hours before, and then finishing off at the last minute. Some fish, for instance, can be seared briefly to brown the day before, then chilled and baked or grilled for a few minutes before serving. The same can apply to some poultry and game dishes, especially prime cuts such as breasts. Many stew-type dishes and soups can be completely cooked ahead and kept in the fridge for a couple of days – and most of these can be frozen (see below). Root vegetables can be char-grilled ahead then blasted with heat at the last minute.

In general, try to slightly *under*cook things if cooking completely ahead. You will have to reheat until piping hot, and you don't want things to overcook and disintegrate. Even if the main ingredient in a meal cannot be cooked in advance – like roast beef, for instance – you can pre- or part-cook its accompaniments, the Yorkshire puds and the roast potatoes. While the meat is resting, you will have plenty of time to bring them up to crisp, golden perfection.

Suggested cooking times and cooking techniques are given for the Aga at the end of each recipe. When the top of the oven is used, obviously cooking on the Aga hotplates is very similar, and so I haven't gone into too much detail there. But occasionally, instead of cooking on the Simmering Plate and losing heat by keeping the lid up for a long time, you can cover and cook something like onions in the Simmering Oven. Bring a sauce, stew or casserole to the boil on the Boiling Plate then cover, transfer to the Simmering Oven and cook until tender. This means that although they take longer to cook, they will not boil over, they don't need to be watched, and they will be beautifully tender. And, most importantly, the Aga will not lose too much heat through the open lids.

Cooling and Chilling

These are vital elements of preparing and cooking ahead. When you have partially or completely cooked something, you want it to cool as quickly as possible before chilling. The first thing to do is simple: take off the lid! One option with a casserole-type dish is to decant it from its one hot cooking pot into two smaller, cold dishes, or a shallow roasting tray. This means that more area is exposed to cool air, but also means extra washing-up, so I'm not too keen. And I don't think you need to use cold water baths or ice. A cool ambient temperature, such as in a larder or pantry, should be sufficient.

Once a dish is cool, it must then be covered, with a lid, clingfilm or foil, and stored in the fridge for the recommended time.

Efficient cooling and chilling are particularly important when you are cooking for a crowd. Larger quantities of food cooked together, because of their density, will take longer to cool. In this case, you may be obliged to decant them into other dishes (get someone else to do the washing-up!).

And if you haven't room enough in your own fridge, ask your friends and neighbours to lend theirs. It's the least they can do if they're coming to eat your delicious food!

Never add a garnish to a cooked dish before chilling and/or freezing. Do so when it is reheated, immediately before serving.

Freezing and Thawing

The freezer can be used very creatively when you are planning, preparing and cooking ahead. Even if you just use it to freeze basics such as butter or bread, you can be one step ahead, in that you don't have to rush to the shops at the last minute. And blanched home-grown green vegetables can be happily frozen.

If you like to cook things fresh at the last moment, there are a number of dishes here that can be prepared – the *Chilean Chicken* on page 69, for example – and frozen raw. Sauces, stocks and soups can be made and frozen well in advance, as can dishes in sauces, such as casseroles or curries. Baked goods can also be frozen very successfully – a huge advantage when someone phones up to invite themselves to tea!

When freezing, always clearly label the dish with a permanent marker pen – the date, the amount it serves and what it is. There is nothing more annoying than finding food in the freezer you have no idea about! You could also add any useful comment you have room for on the label, such as 'specially good', or 'serve with mash' etc. Freeze soup in meal-sized containers – this avoids having to defrost the whole lot for one person. (Don't add the cream to a soup if you are freezing it: do that when you are reheating.) Freeze stock in old cream or yogurt pots – 300–600ml (½–1 pint) plastic pots – then when the recipe states 600ml (1 pint) it is easy to take out just the required amount from the freezer.

When making a complete dish – lasagne or fish pie, say – freeze raw in the dish you are going to cook it in. If you need the dish while it is in the freezer, thaw it for about an hour, loosen the edges, turn out in one solid lump and put in a bag back in the freezer. The dish can then be used and the frozen lasagne can be put back into the dish when it is free again.

Always thaw in the fridge overnight before cooking, and do not cook something in a dish straight from the freezer or the heat of the oven is likely to crack the dish.

Do remember, though, that some things are just not suitable for the freezer. In each of the recipes throughout the book, I give detailed timing instructions, or warn you against.

Reheating and Refreshing

When a dish is taken straight from the fridge, whether it is fully cooked or partially cooked, it will be cold, and therefore could take slightly longer to cook to piping hot – the desired temperature. Use your judgement, and where useful I have mentioned this in the recipe notes. (Incidentally, a thick dish will need its cooking time extended as well.)

If taking an ovenproof porcelain dish straight from the fridge, remember to let it come to room temperature for a little while before cooking, so that the dish doesn't crack from the shock in the oven.

'Refreshing' is the term used for bringing back to life baked goods in general after they have been chilled or defrosted. Breads always taste better when they are warm, but some muffins and scones can taste like new when reheated. It must not be an extreme heat – you don't want to make many things crisp and dry – but just enough to warm the food through thoroughly.

Those, then, are the 'rules'! Now I hope you will enjoy cooking these recipes as much as we have enjoyed testing them. Remember always that cooking should be fun. If you follow my advice about preparing and cooking ahead, I think you will recognise that that is true. Cooking *is* a true pleasure (so long as you are well organised!), and you will be able to relax and enjoy eating with your friends and family.

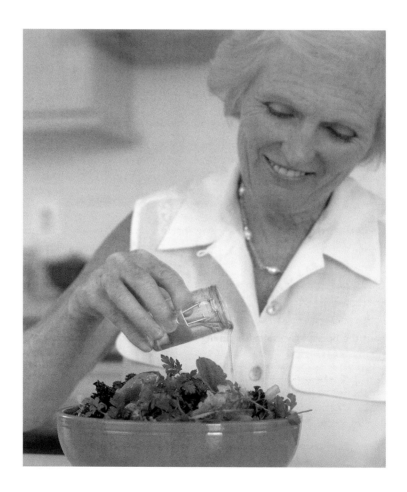

SOUPS AND FIRST COURSES

The starter is the first thing your guests will see and sample, so it must look and taste good. I like to arrange my cold starters on the table ready for when we go into the kitchen or dining room. I think it looks so welcoming – and so organised! This is practical as well, because if the starters have been in the fridge, they always need a little time at room temperature: if food is too cold, you can't taste anything. Cold starters are commonly considered to be the most useful for the cook. They need very little last-minute attention, certainly in the way of cooking, and if the dessert is cold as well, it allows you to spend more time and energy on the main course (usually the high point of any meal) and, most important of all, more time with your guests.

However, hot starters should never be ignored, because if you are organised, and prepare the basics well in advance as I advise here, a final quick heat through in the oven or under the grill – which is all most of them need – is easy. And a hot starter, particularly on a cold winter's day, is always welcome. Soups are perhaps the easiest of the lot, as most can be made at least 1 month in advance and frozen. All you need to do is remember to defrost them overnight, or, at a pinch, melt the frozen block gently in a saucepan. (And I think hot plates for soup are vital: warm soup is *not* the same as hot soup.)

Most of the recipes here are simple to make, although some might seem a little more complicated. But as the method is divided up into separate stages you should never find it too much of a chore. Soufflés, for instance, are said to be the bane of most cooks' lives, but mine can be cooked up to 2 days in advance (actually they can even be frozen), and then given a quick blast in a hot oven to puff them up finally.

And don't forget to serve hot bread or rolls with the first course. You can buy some lovely breads now in bakeries and supermarkets, and warming them through makes most taste even better. If you make the rolls on page 186, freeze them in quantities for the number of guests you expect, then simply defrost and heat.

Smoked Haddock Bouillabaisse

Winter Vegetable Soup **V**

The Very Best Porcini Mushroom Soup **V**

Butternut Squash Soup **V**

Fresh Salmon and Dill Terrines

Garlic-stuffed Grilled Mussels

Char-grilled Vegetables with Goat's Cheese **V**

Individual Baked Artichoke and Parma Ham Galettes

Prawn and Avocado Tians

Crab Cakes with Mild Chilli Sauce

Asparagus and Quail's Egg Salad

Twice-baked Tomato and Feta Soufflés **V**

For more starter ideas, see:

Double Haddock and Herb Fish Cakes (see page 39)

Chilled Mediterranean Salad (see page 94)

Herb Falafels (see page 119)

Onion, Apple and Stilton Little Quiches (see page 120)

Roasted Field Mushrooms with Couscous and Feta (see page 124)

Parisian Red Peppers (see page 127)

Turkey Salad with Avocado, Bacon and Pesto Dressing (see page 141)

Peppadew and Chèvre Crostini (see page 252)

Smoked haddock bouillabaisse

A good substantial soup, a meal in itself served with lots of crusty bread and a salad to follow. I have used full-fat milk to give a good creamy flavour. Add a little cream before serving if you use a low-fat milk.

Serves 6

50g (2 oz) butter

4–6 spring onions, thinly sliced

6 celery sticks, sliced

2 medium carrots, chopped into
  1cm (½ in) dice

450g (1 lb) old potatoes, peeled and cut
  into 2cm (¾ in) chunks

40g (1½ oz) plain flour

600ml (1 pint) fish or vegetable stock

salt and freshly ground black pepper

700g (1½ lb) smoked haddock, skinned
  and chopped into bite-sized pieces

600ml (1 pint) full-fat milk

chopped fresh dill to garnish

1 Heat the butter in a large pan. Add the prepared spring onions, celery and carrots, stir to coat the vegetables in the butter, then cover and cook gently until beginning to soften. Add the potatoes and cook for a further 1–2 minutes.

2 Add the flour to the vegetables, stir and then add the stock. Add black pepper to taste, but no salt at this stage as the fish is very salty. Bring to the boil and simmer until the vegetables are tender, about 10–15 minutes.

3 Add the haddock and milk to the vegetable mixture in the pan and simmer gently for 5–10 minutes until the fish is cooked.

4 Adjust the seasoning and garnish with dill.

cook now, eat later

TO PREPARE AND COOK AHEAD Complete the soup but don't add the garnish yet. Cool, pour into a suitable container and keep in the fridge for 24 hours. Reheat until piping hot.

TO FREEZE Not suitable.

TO COOK IN THE AGA Start on the Boiling Plate. When the vegetables and stock are added, cover and bring to the boil. Transfer to the Simmering Oven and cook until the vegetables are tender. Add the haddock and milk and simmer on the Simmering Plate for about 5 minutes. Continue with the recipe.

Clockwise from top left: The Very Best Porcini Mushroom Soup;
Butternut Squash Soup; Smoked Haddock Bouillabaisse

Winter vegetable soup V

This is a lovely home-made soup, using all vegetables in season, and has been our favourite soup this winter. It is delicious as a first course when there's not much to follow, or for lunch on a cold winter's day. If you are in a hurry, use a food processor to chop the vegetables, but be sure to leave them quite chunky.

Serves 6

50g (2 oz) butter

2 small red onions, finely chopped

2 leeks, finely chopped

3 celery sticks, finely sliced

2 large garlic cloves, crushed

4 level tablespoons plain flour

500ml (18 fl oz) tomato passata

2 large potatoes, peeled and finely diced

1 × 400g can chopped tomatoes

1–2 level tablespoons caster sugar

2 tablespoons tomato purée

1.1 litres (2 pints) chicken or
   vegetable stock

salt and freshly ground black pepper

chopped fresh parsley

1 Melt the butter in a large saucepan and add the onions, leeks, celery and garlic. Stir over a high heat for a few minutes, then lower the heat, cover the pan and cook gently for about 10 minutes to soften.

2 Whisk the flour with a quarter of the passata in a bowl until well blended and smooth. Add the remaining passata.

3 Add the potatoes, tomatoes, sugar and tomato purée to the pan. Blend in the passata and the stock, stir and allow to thicken. Bring to the boil and season. Cover and cook over a gentle heat for about 20–30 minutes or until the vegetables are tender.

4 Check seasoning and serve hot, scattered with plenty of parsley.

cook now, eat later

TO PREPARE AND COOK AHEAD Cool the soup after step 3, cover and store in the fridge for up to 3 days. Bring to the boil and scatter parsley on top to serve.

TO FREEZE Pour the soup into a freezer container, cool, cover and freeze for up to 1 month. Thaw at room temperature for about 8 hours, or overnight in the fridge.

TO COOK IN THE AGA At step 1, cook the vegetables covered in the Simmering Oven for about 10 minutes to soften. Return the pan to the Simmering Oven at step 3, cover and cook for about 15–30 minutes until the vegetables are tender.

The very best porcini mushroom soup ^V

Mushroom soup is a classic, but there are very few tasty ones with intense flavour. Older mushrooms will give the soup a better colour and flavour, and they are sometimes sold off more cheaply. You will find it easier to strain off the mushroom and onion into a sieve and just process the vegetables, adding a little of the liquid rather than lots of batches. Return to the pan with the strained liquid.

Serves 6–8

20–25g (¾–1 oz) dried porcini (cep) mushrooms	75ml (⅛ pint) white wine
150ml (¼ pint) water	1.7 litres (3 pints) good chicken, turkey or vegetable stock
40g (1½ oz) butter	salt and freshly ground black pepper
2 large Spanish onions, finely chopped	2 tablespoons dark soy sauce
2 large garlic cloves, crushed	1 teaspoon lemon juice
700g (1½ lb) open mushrooms, roughly sliced	3 tablespoons double cream
75g (3 oz) plain flour	3 tablespoons sherry (optional)
	lots of chopped fresh parsley

1 Soak the porcini mushrooms for 30 minutes in the water.

2 Melt the butter in a deep saucepan, add the onions and fry on a high heat for a few minutes, without colouring. Lower the heat, cover the pan and cook gently for about 10 minutes until the onion is tender. Add the garlic and open mushrooms and fry over a high heat, stirring all the time, for a further 2–3 minutes.

3 Measure the flour, wine and a small amount of cold stock into a bowl and whisk until smooth.

4 Remove the pan from the heat and slowly stir in the flour mixture and the rest of the stock, stirring until well blended and smooth. Bring to the boil for a couple of minutes until thickened, then add the porcini mushrooms and their carefully strained soaking liquid. Season with salt, pepper, soy sauce and lemon juice. Cover and simmer gently for 15–20 minutes.

5 Allow to cool slightly (until safe enough to handle). Transfer to a food processor and blend until smooth. The soup will not be completely smooth, but will still have some texture from the mushrooms.

6 Check the seasoning and stir in the cream and sherry (if using). Garnish generously with chopped parsley, and serve with some warm crusty bread.

recipe continued overleaf

cook now, eat later

TO PREPARE AND COOK AHEAD Before adding the cream or parsley, allow the soup to cool, transfer to a container and keep in the fridge for up to 3 days. Reheat until piping hot, then add the cream and parsley and serve.

TO FREEZE Cool, pack and freeze the soup, before adding the parsley or cream, for up to a month. Thaw the soup at room temperature for about 8 hours or overnight in the fridge. Or if you are in a hurry, put the frozen block of soup in a pan over a low heat, stirring!

TO COOK IN THE AGA Make the soup in the same way as above, cooking the onion covered in a pan in the Simmering Oven for about 20 minutes in step 2, and 15–20 minutes covered in the Simmering Oven, in step 4.

TIP Cep and porcini mushrooms are the same – 'cep' or 'cèpe' is French in origin, and 'porcini' is Italian. They can be found fresh, but are mostly available dried. They add intense flavour to soups and stews, usually soaked for about 20–30 minutes in warm water before cooking. Add the soaking liquid too as this has a wonderfully intense flavour (strain it well to get rid of any grit).

Butternut squash soup ᵛ

Unlike pumpkins, butternut squashes are available all year. Shaped like a large pear, they have a sweet orange flesh. Roasting them first in the oven means that you don't have to tackle removing the tough skin, and it fills the kitchen with a delicious aroma!

Serves 6

3 small butternut squashes, about 1.6kg (3½ lb) total weight	2 large celery sticks, sliced
about 2 tablespoons olive oil	1 × 2.5cm (1 in) piece fresh root ginger, grated
salt and freshly ground black pepper	1.1–1.3 litres (2–2¼ pints) vegetable or chicken stock
freshly grated nutmeg	
25g (1 oz) butter	a sprig of fresh rosemary or 1 teaspoon dried rosemary
1 large onion, roughly chopped	
2 large carrots, roughly chopped	

Preheat the oven to 200°C/400°F/Gas 6.

1 Cut the butternut squashes in half lengthways. Scoop out the seeds with a metal spoon and discard. Arrange the squash halves cut side up in a roasting tin just big enough to hold them in a single layer, and drizzle over the olive oil. Season the squash halves with salt, pepper and nutmeg. Pour 150ml (¼ pint) water around the squash halves. Cook in the preheated oven for about 1¼ hours, basting occasionally, until very tender. Allow to cool.

2 Melt the butter in a large pan and add the onion, carrot, celery and ginger. Cook for 5–10 minutes until beginning to soften. Add the stock, rosemary and seasoning, bring to the boil then partially cover and simmer for about 20 minutes until the vegetables are tender.

3 When cool enough to handle scoop the flesh from the squash halves and add to the pan. Blend the vegetables in a liquidiser or food processor until smooth. (If you use a food processor, it is easier to process the vegetables with a little of the liquid, adding the remaining liquid to the processed vegetables to make the soup.)

4 Taste for seasoning and serve hot with crusty bread.

cook now, eat later

TO PREPARE AND COOK AHEAD Allow to cool, transfer to a suitable container, cover and keep in the fridge for up to 3 days. Reheat thoroughly to serve.

TO FREEZE Cool the soup at the end of step 3. Pack and freeze for up to 3 months. Thaw at room temperature for 8 hours or overnight in the fridge. Reheat thoroughly to serve.

TO COOK IN THE AGA Cook the squash as in step 1 in a roasting tin on the second set of runners in the Roasting Oven for about 1 hour until tender. Cook the first part of step 2 on the Simmering Plate, then add the stock, etc. Bring to the boil on the Boiling Plate for about 4 minutes, cover and transfer to the Simmering Oven for about 20 minutes. Continue with the recipe.

Fresh salmon and dill terrines

These terrines are impressive and very easy to make – no gelatine! Don't expect them to set firm, it is a soft and light consistency. They can be made a day ahead in small round or oval ramekins or indeed avocado dishes at a push.

Serves 6

350g (12 oz) fresh salmon fillet (boned weight)	6 tablespoons full-fat crème fraîche
salt and freshly ground black pepper	2 tablespoons chopped fresh dill
6 small sprigs of fresh dill	juice of ½ lemon
3 slices smoked salmon	
6 tablespoons 'light' low-calorie mayonnaise	TO SERVE
	a few salad leaves, dressed
	6 lemon wedges

Preheat the oven to 160°C/325°F/Gas 3.

1 Season the fresh salmon with salt and pepper and wrap in one layer of buttered foil. Slide on to a baking sheet and bake until just opaque, about 10 minutes. Remove any skin (but keep any juice which has come out of the fish). Allow to cool to lukewarm.

2 Wet the inside of 6 small ramekins and line with clingfilm. Place a sprig of dill in the base of each and cut 6 discs of smoked salmon to fit neatly into the base on top of the dill. (If there is not enough smoked salmon to make 6 complete discs, use the odd pieces to form circles.) Use the base of the ramekin on top of the slice of smoked salmon to judge a circle.

3 Flake the cold salmon fillet, removing any bones. Mix the salmon and any cooked jelly with the mayonnaise and crème fraîche in a bowl, and season with the dill, lemon juice, salt and pepper. Taste and add more seasoning if necessary. Divide evenly between the ramekins and cover with any overhanging clingfilm. Allow to set in the fridge for about 12 hours, preferably overnight.

4 The next day turn out on a few dressed salad leaves. Serve with brown bread and butter.

cook now, eat later

> **TO PREPARE AND COOK AHEAD** Completely make up to 2 days ahead. Keep in the fridge. Turn out up to 2 hours ahead and keep in the fridge until just before serving.
>
> **TO FREEZE** Not suitable.
>
> **TO COOK IN THE AGA** Cook the salmon for about 8 minutes in the Roasting Oven on the lowest set of runners.

Garlic-stuffed grilled mussels

Choose the large, green-lipped New Zealand mussels for this dish. They look stunning and are less fiddly than the normal smaller, blue-grey mussels. They are available pre-cooked from good supermarkets or, of course, you can cook your own.

Serves 6

1kg (2¼ lb) green-lipped New Zealand mussels (about 36)	finely grated zest of 1 lemon
	2 tablespoons chopped fresh parsley
about 50ml (2 fl oz) water or white wine	salt and freshly ground black pepper
a knob of butter	about 25g (1 oz) Parmesan, grated
1 small onion, finely chopped	a little paprika for dusting
2 garlic cloves, crushed	
3 fresh tomatoes	TO SERVE
about 75g (3 oz) fresh white breadcrumbs	a little salad of baby spinach leaves, lightly dressed

1 If the mussels need cooking, wash in plenty of cold water, scraping away any barnacles and pulling off the beards. Discard any mussels that are open and which do not close when tapped sharply. Put the mussels and water or wine into a large pan, cover and cook over a high heat for 3–4 minutes, shaking the pan occasionally, until the mussels have just opened. (Discard any that remain closed.) Drain the mussels, then break off and discard the empty half shells. Put the mussels still in the outer shell in a single layer on a baking tray.

2 Melt the butter in a small pan, add the onion and garlic and cook gently until soft but not coloured.

3 Skin the tomatoes, cut in half, remove the seeds and chop the flesh finely.

4 Mix the breadcrumbs with the onion and garlic, tomato, lemon zest, parsley and season with salt and pepper.

5 Top each mussel with about a teaspoon of stuffing, sprinkle with Parmesan and dust with paprika.

6 Grill under a hot preheated grill for about 3–5 minutes, or until they are crisp and golden brown. Serve immediately on a bed of dressed fresh baby spinach.

cook now, eat later

TO PREPARE AND COOK AHEAD Prepare to the end of step 5 up to 6 hours ahead. Cover and keep in the fridge until needed. Grill to serve until piping hot right through.

TO FREEZE Not suitable.

TO COOK IN THE AGA Use the Boiling Plate for steps 1 and 2. Arrange the stuffed mussels on a baking sheet and slide on to the second set of runners in the Roasting Oven for about 10 minutes or until golden brown and crisp.

Asparagus and quail's egg salad

This attractive plate of salad is light and tempting. You could swap some of the ingredients: salmon for prawns, and perhaps add some dressed artichoke hearts.

Serves 6

12 quail's eggs

18 asparagus spears or, if large, 9 cut in half lengthways (cut off the very woody ends)

2 tablespoons 'light' low-calorie mayonnaise

2 tablespoons half-fat crème fraîche

1 heaped teaspoon finely chopped fresh chives

1 heaped teaspoon finely chopped fresh parsley

salt and freshly ground black pepper

6 slices smoked salmon

1 lemon, cut into 6 wedges

1 Bring the quail's eggs to the boil in cold water and boil for a further 3 minutes. Drain, run under cold water and peel.

2 Cut the asparagus into tips of 5cm (2 in) in length, and the remaining stalks into chunks of just under 1 cm (½ in), peeling first with a potato peeler if the stems are a bit woody. Cook the stems in boiling water for 4–5 minutes, adding the tips during the final 2 minutes. Drain and refresh thoroughly in very cold water.

3 Measure the mayonnaise, crème fraîche and herbs into a bowl with the well-dried asparagus stalks. Season well with salt and pepper.

4 Arrange a slice of smoked salmon around the edge of each starter plate, spoon the mayonnaise and asparagus mixture into the centre of each plate, and top with 4 halved quail's eggs and 3 asparagus tips. Serve with a lemon wedge and brown bread.

cook now, eat later

TO PREPARE AND COOK AHEAD If you have room in your fridge, assemble completely on individual plates, cover tightly and keep in the fridge for up to 12 hours. Or complete steps 1–3, cover and keep in the fridge for up to 6 hours.

TO FREEZE Not suitable.

TIP Quail's eggs are easier to peel if not too fresh, but well within their sell-by date. I boil them for 3 minutes, then plunge them into cold water and peel from the pointed end straightaway. When offering with drinks, pile in a bowl but leave a few with their shells on as this looks more attractive. Serve with celery salt.

Char-grilled sea bass on a bed of vegetables

Supper in one dish. Prepare the vegetables and fish ahead, leaving only a salad to make on the day.

Serves 6

butter	4 large tomatoes, skinned, quartered
700g (1½ lb) new potatoes	and seeded
1 large onion, cut into wedges	4 red peppers, cut in half and seeded
olive oil	50g (2 oz) black olives in oil, drained
1 garlic clove, crushed	6 sea bass fillets, with the skin left on
salt and freshly ground black pepper	chopped fresh parsley and basil

Lightly butter a 25 × 38cm (10 × 15 in) ovenproof dish. Preheat the oven to 200°C/400°F/Gas 6, and preheat the grill.

1 Boil the potatoes and onion in salted water until the potatoes are only just done. Drain and cut the potatoes into even pieces about 2.5cm (1 in) square, or a bit smaller. Return to the pan with the onion, 1–2 tablespoons of the oil, the garlic, salt and pepper.

2 Arrange the potatoes and onion down the centre of a large ovenproof dish, scatter the tomatoes on top, and season with salt and pepper.

3 Put the peppers cut side down on to the grill rack and grill under the hot grill until the skin blisters and blackens. Whilst still hot put the peppers into a polythene bag and seal the top so that they sweat. When cool enough to handle, peel off the skin and cut the flesh into quarters.

4 Mix the peppers with the olives, season and coat with olive oil. Spoon the peppers and olives down either side of the potatoes. Cover with foil.

5 Slash the fish skin and brush with a little oil. Season the fish and fry skin side down in a very hot frying pan or ridged grill pan over high heat for about 1 minute until the skin is crisp and brown. The flesh will still be raw underneath.

6 Reheat the vegetables, covered, in the preheated oven for about 20 minutes, until very steamy and exceedingly hot. Remove the foil.

7 Put the fish on top of the potatoes, skin side up, and bake for about 8–10 minutes until just cooked. Sprinkle with parsley and basil to serve.

recipe continued overleaf

Braemar pheasant

This recipe uses pheasant breasts. Use the legs for a casserole or stock. Leeks and bacon go really well in game recipes.

Serves 6

100g (4 oz) thickly sliced bacon,
   cut into strips
2 leeks, coarsely shredded
2 tablespoons sunflower oil
6 pheasant breasts, skin removed
25g (1 oz) plain flour
300ml (½ pint) apple juice
300ml (½ pint) chicken stock

1 tablespoon cranberry or
   redcurrant jelly
a few sprigs of fresh parsley
1 large sprig of fresh thyme
1 bay leaf
salt and freshly ground black pepper
a generous amount of chopped
   fresh parsley

1 Heat a non-stick frying pan and add the bacon. Cook gently, stirring occasionally, for a few minutes, then add the leeks and cook until the leeks are beginning to brown and the bacon is crisp. Remove the leeks and bacon to a plate.

2 Heat the oil in the same pan and fry the pheasant breasts quickly on a high heat until browned all over. Lift out and add to the bacon and leeks. Add the flour to the pan and cook, stirring, for 1 minute. Gradually blend in the apple juice, stock and cranberry or redcurrant jelly. Bring to the boil, stirring until thickened.

3 Return the browned pheasant, bacon and leeks to the pan, and add the parsley sprigs, thyme, bay and seasoning. Bring to the boil, cover and simmer gently for about 10–15 minutes until the pheasant is tender. Keep warm and rest for 15 minutes before serving.

4 Taste the sauce for seasoning, remove the parsley sprigs, thyme and bay leaf, and sprinkle over lots of chopped parsley to serve. Good with mashed potato.

cook now, eat later

TO PREPARE AND COOK AHEAD Prepare to the end of step 3. Cool quickly, cover and keep in the fridge for up to 1 day. Reheat until piping hot to serve.

TO FREEZE It will freeze but take care not to overcook the pheasant in the first place. Freeze and thaw completely. Reheat until piping hot, stirring.

TO COOK IN THE AGA Cook steps 1 and 2 on the Boiling Plate. At step 3, bring to the boil on the Boiling Plate, cover and transfer to the Simmering Oven for about 10–15 minutes until the pheasant is tender.

Thai fragrant chicken

There is a wonderful light and subtle flavour to this chicken dish. Ideally, it should be made the day before so that the flavours infuse, and then can be reheated gently to serve. We like a generous amount of sauce but if you like less, reduce the amount of stock. It would then also make a thicker sauce, which you may prefer.

Serves 6

5 large chicken breasts, skin and bone removed, cut into thin strips	1 × 2.5cm (1 in) piece cinnamon stick
salt and freshly ground black pepper	seeds of 6 cardamom pods, crushed
2 tablespoons sunflower oil	2 teaspoons ground cumin
1 large onion, finely chopped	1 bay leaf
2 garlic cloves, crushed	150ml (¼ pint) chicken stock
1 × 3cm (1–1½ in) piece fresh root ginger, grated	1 × 200ml carton coconut cream (UHT)
½ teaspoon garam masala	finely grated zest and juice of ½–1 lime
	chopped fresh coriander

1 Season the chicken with salt and pepper. Heat half the oil in a large non-stick pan, add the chicken and quickly brown. Lift out on to a plate. It is best to do this in batches.

2 Heat the remaining oil in the frying pan, then add the onion, garlic and ginger. Cook for a few minutes over a high heat, then cover and cook gently over a low heat for about 10 minutes until soft.

3 Add the garam masala, cinnamon, cardamom, cumin and bay leaf, and stir for 1 minute. Add the browned chicken. Blend in the stock and the coconut cream, stirring continually until it comes to the boil. Season, cover with the lid and simmer gently for about 5 minutes, or until the chicken is cooked. Remove and discard the cinnamon stick and bay leaf. Stir in the lime zest and juice.

4 Sprinkle with coriander, and serve with *Aromatic Thai Rice* (see page 143).

recipe continued overleaf

cook now, eat later

Chicken olives Provençal

This is a super family supper dish. Boneless chicken thighs are readily available from all good supermarkets. The stuffing and sauce are very easy to do and the chicken doesn't need browning ahead.

Serves 4–6

3 large good-quality pork sausages	SAUCE
25g (1 oz) black olives, stoned and	2 tablespoons dark soy sauce
finely chopped	1 scant tablespoon Worcestershire sauce
finely grated zest of 1 lemon	1 tablespoon runny honey
1 tablespoon finely chopped fresh thyme	2 teaspoons grainy mustard
1 tablespoon finely chopped fresh sage	1 × 400g can chopped tomatoes
salt and freshly ground black pepper	
8 chicken thighs, skin and bone removed	
25g (1 oz) Parmesan, coarsely grated	
chopped fresh parsley to garnish	

You will need an ovenproof dish about 28 × 23cm (11 × 9 in). Preheat the oven to 190°C/375°F/Gas 5.

❙ Slit each sausage skin lengthways and remove the meat. Put the sausagemeat into a bowl, add the olives, lemon zest, thyme, sage, salt and pepper, and mix well.

2 Unfold and lay out the chicken thighs (smooth side down). Season with salt and pepper and fill with a tablespoon of the sausagemeat stuffing (where the bone would have been). Bring each edge of the chicken towards the middle, over the stuffing. Arrange in the dish, join side down. Season the thighs all over.

3 Blend together the sauce ingredients in a bowl and pour over the thighs, ensuring all are covered. Sprinkle Parmesan over the chicken.

4 Cook in the preheated oven for about 30–40 minutes until the chicken is tender and the sauce is piping hot.

5 Garnish with parsley and serve with herby mashed potatoes.

cook now, eat later

TO PREPARE AND COOK AHEAD Complete to the end of step 3, cover and keep in the fridge for up to 8 hours. Cook as directed in step 4, ensuring that the chicken is cooked and the sauce is piping hot before serving. Or complete to the end of step 4, cool quickly, cover and keep in the fridge for up to 24 hours. Reheat at 200°C/400°F/Gas 6 for about 20–25 minutes, or until the chicken and sauce are piping hot.

TO FREEZE The raw stuffed chicken thighs freeze very successfully. Defrost thoroughly in the fridge overnight before cooking, as from step 4. Or freeze the cooked completed dish. Thaw for 6 hours at room temperature or overnight in the fridge. To reheat, follow the above.

TO COOK IN THE AGA For step 4, slide the dish on to the second set of runners in the Roasting Oven for about 25–30 minutes, or until the chicken is tender and the sauce boiling.

Chilean chicken

A quick and easy dish that looks good enough to serve for a dinner party. There is no sauce to make at the last minute, as the savoury butter can be poured over.

Serves 6

6 chicken breasts, skin and bone removed	SAVOURY BUTTER
salt and freshly ground black pepper	115g (4½ oz) butter
a few fresh coriander leaves to garnish	2–3 hot red chillies, seeded
	3 sun-dried tomatoes in oil, drained
	1 large garlic clove, peeled
	a small bunch of fresh coriander

Preheat the oven to 220°C/425°F/Gas 7.

1 Place all the savoury butter ingredients, plus some salt and pepper, in a food processor and blend until well mixed and almost smooth. Chill if time allows.

2 Beat out the chicken breasts between 2 sheets of clingfilm until thin, using a rolling pin.

3 Reserve a small amount of the savoury butter. Season the chicken breasts with salt and pepper and spread the butter over them. Roll up tightly (like a beef olive) lengthways.

4 Take 6 pieces of foil, big enough to enclose one chicken breast in each. Rub any reserved butter over the foil and put a chicken breast on to each piece. Season again, then fold the foil around the chicken and seal at the side by crimping together.

5 Put the chicken parcels on to a baking tray and cook in the preheated oven for about 20 minutes, depending on the size of the chicken breasts, until cooked. Allow to rest for a further 10 minutes.

6 Lift out of the foil, slice the chicken breasts on the diagonal, and spoon over the buttery juices. Garnish with coriander and serve with rice.

recipe continued overleaf

MEAT

Meat stews and casseroles can, like poultry dishes, be completely cooked ahead and chilled for a day or so, or frozen. They should be cooked until tender, but never overcooked, or the meat chunks could fall apart when reheated. Again as with chicken, tasting is vital, especially when cooking ahead. Taste, then adjust the seasoning as appropriate, but not just with salt and pepper. If something has a lot of tomatoes in it, you may need a pinch of sugar. Perhaps some lemon juice or redcurrant jelly may be needed. You as the host are the first to start when your friends come for a meal, and how sad it would be if your first mouthful alerted you to the fact that you should have added some balsamic vinegar, more pepper or a dash of lemon, or enriched it with some cream.

It's not a fallacy that some meat and poultry dishes just do taste better when reheated. The flavours, especially of spicy dishes and those containing red wine, have time to mature and come together. And even with dishes that cannot be fully prepared ahead, some flavour advantages can be gained: a stuffing can flavour raw meat during an overnight chilling, and a marinade can add flavour and tenderise it at the same time.

I have included some roasts here which of course cannot be cooked ahead – but elements of the individual dishes can (Yorkshire pudding and roast potatoes, for instance), and this will help you have more time when you need it. Even just ordering the meat well in advance from your butcher, particularly of a less common cut such as saddle of lamb, will save you time in a sense. And you can store prime cuts in the fridge for a few days, which will allow them to mature and gain even more flavour. (Remove the butcher's plastic, and rewrap in greaseproof paper, or non-stick parchment paper.)

Marinated Roast Lamb with Minted Couscous and Whisky Gravy

Roast Saddle of Lamb with Rosemary and Redcurrant Gravy

Mexican Spicy Lamb

Tagine of Lamb

Pork Escalopes with Apple and Onion

Roast Pork Fillets with Apple and Fennel Sauce

Roast Prime Rib of Beef with Beetroot and Horseradish

Pan-fried Fillet Steaks with Fresh Herb Sauce

Venison and Beef with Port and Apricots

Calf's Liver with Caramelised Onions and Balsamic Gravy

For more meat ideas, see:

Thai Pork Curry (see page 144)

Baked Sausages with Double Onion Marmalade (see page 145)

Glazed Apple Gammon (see page 189)

The Perfect Whole Roast Fillet of Beef with Thyme (see page 198)

Steak and Mushroom Pie with Dauphinoise Potato Topping (see page 200)

Lancashire Lamb Shanks (see page 202)

Mexican spicy lamb

A warming casserole. Serve with tomato and basil salad and chunky garlic bread. Double up for a crowd, adding more cans of beans if they have very healthy appetites. If you have difficulty in getting black-eyed beans, use red kidney beans instead. For the young, use baked beans!

Serves 6–8

900g (2 lb) neck fillet of lamb
2 tablespoons sunflower oil
2 garlic cloves, crushed
1 large onion, sliced
2 level tablespoons plain flour
1 teaspoon ground cumin
1 teaspoon ground coriander
150ml (¼ pint) white wine
1 × 400g can chopped tomatoes

2 level tablespoons tomato purée
salt and freshly ground black pepper
2 × 400g can black-eyed beans
2 generous tablespoons mango chutney

TO SERVE
sprigs of fresh coriander or mint
1 × 150g carton Greek yogurt

Preheat the oven to 160°C/325°F/Gas 3.

1 Remove excess fat from the lamb and cut the flesh into large cubes. Heat half the oil in a large pan, add the lamb and brown in batches, keeping the heat high. Remove the lamb with a slotted spoon on to a plate.

2 Lower the heat and add the remaining oil and the garlic and onion to the pan. Allow to soften for a few minutes, then blend in the flour and spices and allow to cook for a further 2 minutes.

3 Add the wine, tomatoes and tomato purée to the pan along with the meat. Bring to the boil, season with salt and pepper, cover and transfer to the preheated oven for about 2 hours, until the meat is tender.

4 Drain and rinse the beans, add to the lamb with the mango chutney, and cook for about 10 minutes longer. Check the seasoning and tenderness.

5 Garnish with sprigs of coriander or mint. Serve with Greek yogurt seasoned and then mixed with 2 teaspoons chopped coriander or mint if liked.

recipe continued overleaf

Chilled Mediterranean salad ᵛ

A colourful salad to enjoy in summer. It's essential that you serve it chilled. It's also good on individual plates as a summer first course, nice with warm bread or rolls.

Serves 6

550g (1¼ lb) ripe tomatoes
(about 6 large)
salt and freshly ground black pepper
1 medium cucumber
1 small mild onion
1 medium red pepper
2 small Little Gem lettuces, broken in
small pieces
2 tablespoons roughly chopped fresh
flat-leaf parsley
leaves from a few sprigs of fresh basil
about 18 black olives (optional)
a few shavings of Parmesan

CROÛTONS
2 slices thick white bread, crust removed
2 tablespoons good olive oil
2 fat garlic cloves, crushed

DRESSING
3 tablespoons good olive oil
1 tablespoon lemon juice
1 teaspoon caster sugar
1 tablespoon balsamic vinegar

1 Slice off the ends of the tomatoes thinly and cut each tomato into 3 slices then slice each round into about 6 wedges. Transfer to a fairly large bowl, season with pepper but don't stir as the tomatoes will break up.

2 Cut the cucumber in half lengthways. Remove the seeds with a melon baller or teaspoon or simply push your thumb nail firmly down the centre of the cucumber from one end to the other. Discard the seeds. Cut the cucumber in slices about the thickness of medium-sliced bread. Add the horseshoe cucumber shapes to the bowl.

3 Peel and cut the onion in 4 then cut each wedge into very fine slices (not cutting through the root) which will fall apart into bow shapes. Add to the bowl.

4 Seed the pepper and cut into fine julienne strips. Add with the lettuce to the bowl but do not mix together. Cover with clingfilm and chill for 6 hours ideally.

5 Meanwhile, make the croûtons and dressing. Cut the bread into rough cubes, and put in a polythene bag with the oil, garlic and a little pepper. Gently shake to evenly coat with the oil. Either put in a foil-lined grill pan and toast under the grill until golden, or brown in a hot oven (about 220°C/425°F/Gas 7), watching carefully.

recipe continued overleaf

Spiced lentil and tomato moussaka ^V

You need not be a vegetarian to enjoy this dish. It is rich in flavour and, with the added red peppers and tomatoes, colourful too. Buy dried French Puy lentils in packets, and add as they are.

Serves 6

6 tablespoons olive oil
2 large onions, roughly chopped
3 large garlic cloves, crushed
2 large red peppers, seeded and
   chopped into large pieces
225g (8 oz) dried Puy lentils
3 × 400g cans chopped tomatoes
300ml (½ pint) vegetable stock
1–2 tablespoons mango chutney
salt and freshly ground black pepper
3 large aubergines, thickly sliced,
   about 5mm (¼ in)

CHEESE SAUCE
50g (2 oz) butter
50g (2 oz) plain flour
600ml (1 pint) milk
225g (8 oz) mature Cheddar, grated
2 teaspoons Dijon mustard
freshly grated nutmeg to taste

Preheat the oven to 200°C/400°F/Gas 6, and lightly grease a large, shallow, ovenproof dish, about 25 × 33cm (10 × 13 in).

1 Heat 2 tablespoons of the olive oil in a large sauté pan. Add the onions, garlic and peppers and cook gently for about 4–5 minutes until beginning to soften.

2 Add the lentils, tomatoes, vegetable stock, mango chutney and seasoning. Cover and simmer for about 40–60 minutes or until the lentils are cooked. Check the seasoning.

3 Brush the sliced aubergines with the remaining olive oil and season with salt and pepper. Arrange in a single layer (you will have to do this in batches) on a baking sheet and place under a hot grill for about 2–3 minutes each side, until the slices are golden brown.

4 Next make the cheese sauce. Melt the butter in a medium saucepan, take off the heat and stir in the flour. Return to a low heat, stirring for 2–3 minutes, then again remove from the heat and gradually add the milk. Bring up to the boil, stirring, and simmer for about 2 minutes. Add 175g (6 oz) of the cheese, the mustard, nutmeg and some salt and pepper.

recipe continued overleaf

Mediterranean vegetable galette with mozzarella V

A delicious puff pastry case filled with stir-fried vegetables. Ready-rolled puff pastry is easy to buy and even easier to use! The pastry border around the edge will rise up and frame the vegetables like a picture. It is essential to preheat the baking sheet as the bottom heat is needed to brown the pastry underneath the vegetables.

Serves 6

1 × 375g (13 oz) packet ready-rolled
  puff pastry
1 egg, beaten
fresh basil

FILLING
1 tablespoon olive oil
1 small aubergine, cut in half lengthways
  and thinly sliced
1 red onion, finely sliced

1 red pepper and 1 yellow pepper,
  seeded and cut into 2.5cm (1 in)
  cubes
1 small garlic clove, crushed
salt and freshly ground black pepper
100g (4 oz) Philadelphia full-fat
  cream cheese
1 tablespoon pesto
50g (2 oz) cherry tomatoes, halved
75g (3 oz) mozzarella cheese,
  coarsely grated

Preheat the oven to 220°C/425°F/Gas 7. Put a large heavy baking sheet on a high shelf in the oven to preheat.

1 Heat the oil in a deep frying pan, and stir-fry the aubergine until golden brown. Add the onion, peppers and garlic, and continue to stir-fry for about 5–10 minutes until the peppers are just cooked. Make sure that all the moisture has been driven off, over a high heat if necessary, otherwise the pastry will be soggy. Season with salt and pepper. Set aside to cool.

2 Take the ready-rolled puff pastry and roll out a little bigger to a fairly thin rectangle – about 25.5 × 38cm (10 × 15 in). Transfer to a hot baking sheet and score a 4cm (1½ in) border around the edge of the rectangle (score with a knife half-way through the pastry, do not cut right through). Using a sharp knife, diagonally mark around the border about every inch to give a pretty edge (again, do not cut right through). Prick the base of the pastry inside the border.

3 Mix the cream cheese in a bowl with the pesto and season with salt and pepper. Spread the cream cheese mixture evenly over the raw pastry, inside the marked border. Pile the cooled, cooked vegetables over the top of the cream cheese (again ensuring all is inside the border). Arrange the tomatoes (cut side up) on top of the vegetables and scatter over the mozzarella. Brush the pastry border with a little beaten egg.

recipe continued overleaf

Parisian red peppers V

Ideal for a light lunch. Serve with crusty bread to soak up the juices and perhaps a green salad. Mozzarella can be used instead of halloumi.

Serves 6

6 large red peppers
salt and freshly ground black pepper
2 tablespoons olive oil
1 medium onion, finely chopped
1 garlic clove, crushed
225g (8 oz) chestnut mushrooms, sliced
2 × 300g cans flageolet beans, rinsed and
    drained

about 24 black olives, stoned
about 2 tablespoons roughly chopped
    fresh basil
2 × 250g packs halloumi cheese, coarsely
    grated
fresh basil leaves to garnish

Preheat the oven to 180°C/350°F/Gas 4. Lightly oil a large, shallow ovenproof dish, large enough to fit 12 pepper halves snugly in a single layer (or two smaller shallow dishes).

1 Cut the peppers in half lengthways, leaving the green stalk but removing the seeds. Put into the ovenproof dish and season lightly.

2 Heat the oil in a medium pan, add the onion and garlic and cook gently for 5–10 minutes until soft. Add the mushrooms and continue to cook until tender. Add the beans and olives to the pan and season to taste.

3 Divide the bean and mushroom mixture between the pepper halves, scatter with the chopped basil and top with the cheese.

4 Bake in the preheated oven for about 1 hour until the peppers are tender and the cheese golden and bubbling. Scatter with basil leaves to serve.

cook now, eat later

TO PREPARE AND COOK AHEAD Cook and cool the mushroom and bean mixture, then use to fill the peppers. Complete step 3, cover and keep in the fridge for up to 8 hours.

TO FREEZE Not suitable.

TO COOK IN THE AGA Cook the onion and mushrooms on the Boiling Plate. Loosely cover the assembled dish with foil, and slide on to the grid shelf on the floor of the Roasting Oven for about 30 minutes. Remove the foil and cook for a further 20 minutes or until the peppers are tender and the cheese golden and bubbling.

SUPPER DISHES

I included this section because I think a good number of people these days prefer to eat in the kitchen with friends rather than give more formal dinner parties. And of course, when people are milling around you in the kitchen – chatting, laughing, perhaps even trying to help (or interfering!) – you want to be as well organised and as well ahead as possible. You don't want your knife technique to come under criticism, or any unwashed pots to be too much in evidence.

Even if you are offering something that must be cooked at the last moment, you can have prepared part of it beforehand. I've suggested a few pasta recipes here – comfort food, always welcomed by guests of all ages – and, perhaps surprisingly, the pasta can be cooked up to 6 hours in advance. I always use dried pasta when I plan to do this. (In fact I believe the Italians prefer dried pasta to fresh, and that's good enough for me!) What you do is cook the pasta in plenty of boiling salted water until al dente, still with a slight bite in the centre. Refresh in plenty of cold running water. Leave the cold pasta in the colander, and cover with clingfilm. To reheat, either tip the pasta into the hot sauce if the pasta has a sauce with it, or plunge into boiling salted water for a few moments, stirring until the pasta is piping hot. Drain and serve at once.

Foods that need to be crisp should be done at the last moment, but the vegetables for the *Phad Thai Noodles* (see page 138), for instance, can be prepared well ahead, as can the marination of the fajita filling. A bit of stir-frying isn't going to prove too difficult in front of your guests. But otherwise the remainder of the recipes here can be prepared and cooked at least a day before, and then reheated, which allows you to mingle happily with your guests, share a drink with them, and enjoy the evening without any hassle in the kitchen.

Pasta Primavera **V**

Chilli-hot Monkfish Pasta with Vegetables

Penne Pasta with Parma Ham

Pistou Pasta with Rocket **V**

Salmon Coulibiac

Phad Thai Noodles with Seafood

Spicy Turkey Fajitas

Turkey Salad with Avocado, Bacon and Pesto Dressing

Piquant Chicken with Basil

Aromatic Thai Rice **V**

Thai Pork Curry

Baked Sausages with Double Onion Marmalade

For more supper ideas, see:

Individual Baked Artichoke and Parma Ham Galettes (see page 26)

Crab Cakes with Mild Chilli Sauce (see page 30)

Twice-baked Tomato and Feta Soufflés (see page 34)

Double Haddock and Herb Fish Cakes (see page 39)

Moroccan Fish (see page 52)

Chardonnay Chicken with Artichoke Hearts (see page 62)

Chicken Olives Provençal (see page 66)

Mexican Spicy Lamb (see page 80)

Tagine of Lamb (see page 83)

Pork Escalopes with Apple and Onion (see page 84)

Onion, Apple and Stilton Little Quiches (see page 120)

See also Vegetarian Specials (pages 108–127)

Pasta primavera V

A fresh, fairly healthy – and meat-free – pasta recipe, using bright, colourful vegetables.

Serves 6

2 tablespoons olive oil	350g (12 oz) dried tagliatelle
2 large onions, halved and thickly sliced	225g (8 oz) broccoli florets
2 red peppers, seeded and cut into	225g (8 oz) asparagus tips
large pieces	200ml (7 fl oz) crème fraîche
salt and freshly ground black pepper	3–4 tablespoons pesto, according
350g (12 oz) small courgettes,	to taste
thickly sliced	50g (2 oz) Parmesan, freshly grated

Preheat the oven to 220°C/425°F/Gas 7.

1 Measure the oil into a large polythene bag, add the onions and red peppers and season well. Toss together, then turn into a large roasting tin and roast in the preheated oven, turning from time to time, for about 40 minutes, until the vegetables are just done. Add the courgettes after 20 minutes as they take less time to cook.

2 Boil the pasta in salted water according to the instructions on the packet, usually about 10 minutes, adding the broccoli and asparagus for the last 3 minutes. Drain and leave in the colander while making the sauce.

3 Heat the crème fraîche and pesto together in the pasta saucepan. Return the pasta and roasted vegetables to the pan, and toss together, adding some of the Parmesan.

4 Serve immediately in a heated dish, sprinkled with the remaining Parmesan.

cook now, eat later

TO PREPARE AND COOK AHEAD The roast vegetables can be roasted well ahead of time, or even the day before, and reheated in a hot oven as you boil the pasta. If liked, the pasta can be cooked, drained, refreshed and covered up to 6 hours in advance. As can the broccoli and asparagus: boil in salted water for 3 minutes then plunge into cold water and drain.

TO FREEZE Not suitable.

TO COOK IN THE AGA Roast the onions and red peppers on the floor of the Roasting Oven for 30 minutes, turning from time to time, until just done. Add the courgettes after 15 minutes. Cook all else on the Boiling Plate.

Pistou pasta with rocket V

A very simple recipe, which will take just 15 minutes to make from scratch — but you can prepare ahead as well. Serve with a green leaf salad.

Serves 6

350g (12 oz) dried penne pasta	coarsely grated Parmesan to serve
150ml (¼ pint) white wine	
2 shallots, finely chopped	PISTOU
450g (1 lb) mixed varieties of wild mushrooms, coarsely sliced	a very good handful of fresh basil (leaves and stalks)
salt and freshly ground black pepper	1 fat garlic clove, peeled
4 tablespoons pouring double cream	rocket stalks (see above)
1 × 50g (2 oz) bag rocket, removing some of the end stalks to add to the pistou	about 4 tablespoons olive oil

1 First boil a pan of salted water for the pasta. When boiling, add the pasta and cook for about 12 minutes or according to packet instructions.

2 Then make the pistou. Measure the basil, garlic and rocket stalks into a food processor and quickly process. Then add the olive oil and process again. The oil doesn't mix well, but it takes on the flavour of the garlic and herbs.

3 Boil the wine in a large frying pan with the shallots and reduce for a few minutes. Add all of the mushrooms and stir over a high heat for a few minutes until the mushrooms are cooked and the liquid has reduced to 2 tablespoons. Season with salt and pepper. Add the cream and pistou, stirring to mix.

4 Drain the pasta and add to the mushroom mixture in the pan. Check the seasoning.

5 At the last moment stir in the rocket leaves, then serve with the Parmesan.

cook now, eat later

TO PREPARE AND COOK AHEAD Chop the shallots and slice the mushrooms up to 8 hours ahead. Make the pistou, cover and keep in the fridge for up to 24 hours. You could cook, drain, refresh, cover and chill the pasta up to 6 hours ahead.

TO FREEZE Not suitable.

TO COOK IN THE AGA Use the Boiling Plate to cook the mushrooms and the pasta.

Phad Thai noodles with seafood

A healthy fresh recipe, inspired by my much admired friend Ken Hom, the king of Chinese and Eastern cooking.

Serves 6

175g (6 oz) Thai rice noodles or fine egg noodles

150g (5 oz) sugar-snap peas, cut thinly on the diagonal

2 tablespoons sunflower oil

1 garlic clove, crushed

1 x 2.5cm (1 in) piece fresh root ginger, finely grated

2 red chillies, seeded and finely chopped

150g (5 oz) shiitake mushrooms, sliced

1 leek, sliced lengthways into thin batons

100g (4 oz) baby sweetcorn, cut into 4 lengthways

100g (4 oz) beansprouts

375g (12 oz) mixed seafood (i.e. fresh prawns, scallops, squid)

2 tablespoons sherry

4 tablespoons soy sauce

2 tablespoons oyster sauce

2 tablespoons lime juice

a few salted peanuts (optional) and sliced spring onions to garnish

1 Cook the noodles according to the packet instructions. For the last minute add the sugar-snap peas to the noodle pan. Drain and refresh lightly.

2 Heat the oil in a large frying pan or wok over a high heat until very hot. Add the garlic, ginger and chillies and fry for 2–3 minutes. Add the mushrooms, leek, baby corn and beansprouts and stir-fry for about 5 minutes.

3 When the vegetables are nearly cooked, add the seafood to the pan with the sherry, soy and oyster sauces and lime juice.

4 When the seafood is cooked through, stir in the noodles and sugar-snap peas, and mix well over a low heat for a few minutes.

5 Turn into a serving dish, and garnish with peanuts, if using, and spring onions.

cook now, eat later

TO PREPARE AHEAD Chop all the vegetables, cover and keep in the fridge until needed, up to 8 hours ahead. Stir-fry just before serving.

TO FREEZE Not suitable.

TO COOK IN THE AGA Boil the noodles and stir-fry the vegetables on the Boiling Plate.

Apricot brioche tart V

A wonderfully quick and easy tart, which is good made with canned pears as well. If I was giving a numerical rating to this recipe, I would give 10 out of 10!

Serves 6–8

1 egg

2 tablespoons caster sugar

1 × 250g tub mascarpone cheese

about 225g (8 oz) brioche, sliced about
  1cm (½ in) thick from a loaf

2 × 400g (14 oz) cans apricot halves,
  drained

about 4 tablespoons demerara sugar

icing sugar for dusting

Lightly grease an ovenproof, shallow-sided dish, about 28cm (11 in) in diameter. Preheat the oven to 180°C/350°F/Gas 4.

1 Lightly whisk the egg and caster sugar together in a bowl. Add the mascarpone and whisk again until smooth and there are no lumps.

2 Arrange the brioche slices as neatly as possible in a single layer on the greased dish to completely cover it. Trim the brioche slices as necessary to fit. Spread the mascarpone mixture over the brioche slices to about 1cm (½ in) away from the edge. (You don't have to be accurate about this!)

3 Arrange the apricot halves neatly in circles over the mascarpone right to the edge of the brioche. Sprinkle the demerara sugar over the apricots.

4 Bake in the preheated oven for about 30–35 minutes until the custard is set and golden. Serve immediately with crème fraîche, and dust with icing sugar.

cook now, eat later

TO PREPARE AND COOK AHEAD Step 1 can be made and kept in the fridge up to 12 hours before. The brioche can be arranged in the dish, covered tightly for up to 12 hours ahead. The apricots can be drained. Assemble up to 2 hours before serving. Or bake the day before and reheat in the oven preheated to 190°C/375°F/ Gas 5 for about 10 minutes. (It is best cooked just before serving, though.)

TO FREEZE Not suitable.

TO COOK IN THE AGA Bake on the floor of the Roasting Oven for about 8 minutes then slide on to the top set of runners in the Roasting Oven for a further 12 minutes until the custard is set and golden.

Apple, lemon and cinnamon strudel V

An apple strudel used to be such a popular recipe, and we think it's worth a comeback. It is so quick and easy to make too. The breadcrumbs help to absorb some of the liquid from the apples, and stop the pastry going soggy.

Serves 6

about 6 sheets filo pastry (if the pastry is
   very thin, use 9 sheets)
about 50g (2 oz) butter, melted
about 25g (1 oz) fresh breadcrumbs

FILLING
1 large cooking apple (about 400g/14 oz
   peeled weight), peeled, cored and
   sliced

finely grated zest and juice of ½ lemon
50g (2 oz) demerara sugar
1 teaspoon mixed spice
1 teaspoon ground cinnamon
50g (2 oz) sultanas

ICING
a little lemon juice
175g (6 oz) icing sugar, sieved

Lightly grease a baking tray. Preheat the oven to 190°C/375°F/Gas 5.

1 Mix all the filling ingredients together in a bowl.

2 Place 3 sheets of filo, long sides together, side by side on a board, slightly overlapping in the middle where they join. They should measure altogether about 45 × 31cm (18 × 12 in). Brush with melted butter. Repeat with another 1 or 2 layers, buttering in between the pastry, using the total of 6 or 9 sheets. Sprinkle the top sheets with the breadcrumbs.

3 Spoon the filling into a third of the rectangle at the bottom of one end of the pastry (across the join) about 5cm (2 in) away from the edge and side. Cut away about 2.5cm (1 in) of pastry at the sides, from the top of the filling upwards (this helps prevent too much pastry being folded together).

4 Turn the sides in over the filling and roll up from the filling end into a sausage shape. Carefully lift the strudel on to the baking tray and brush all over with melted butter.

5 Bake in the preheated oven for about 35–40 minutes until the pastry is golden and crisp.

6 Mix the lemon juice with the sieved icing sugar to blend together (do not make it too runny or it will slide off the strudel). Spread or drizzle in a zig-zag pattern over the top of the strudel. Serve immediately with a good vanilla ice-cream or crème fraîche.

recipe continued overleaf

Caramelised peaches with brandy ^V

The peaches can also be left whole for this recipe, when they look particularly tempting and delicious.

Serves 6

6 fresh peaches or nectarines	ground cinnamon
soft butter	brandy
demerara sugar	crème fraîche to serve

Preheat the oven to 200°C/400°F/Gas 6.

1 Peel the peaches or nectarines by dipping into boiling water until the skin is easy to remove (as you would skin a tomato). Cut in half and remove the stones. Dry with kitchen paper, then rub the rounded side of each peach or nectarine with soft butter.

2 Pack the peaches or nectarines cut side down into a dish in which they fit tightly. Sprinkle with demerara sugar and cinnamon and pour about 6 tablespoons of brandy into the dish around them.

3 Bake in the preheated oven for about 30 minutes until tender.

4 Serve hot with cream or *Brandy Ice-cream* (see page 232).

cook now, eat later

TO PREPARE AND COOK AHEAD Cook up to 12 hours ahead of time, but only for 20 minutes. Cover and store in a cool place for up to 12 hours. Reheat in a hot oven at 200°C/400°F/Gas 6 for about 10–15 minutes. Sprinkle with a little more demerara sugar first.

TO FREEZE Not suitable.

TO COOK IN THE AGA Bake on the top set of runners in the Roasting Oven for about 15 minutes until the peaches or nectarines are tender.

COLD DESSERTS

Every single recipe in this chapter can be made in advance – at least the day before – and indeed the majority can be frozen. This is exactly why cold desserts are so popular, of course: once you have a tray of mousses or a bowl of fruit salad in the fridge, or an ice-cream in the freezer, you can forget completely about one course of your meal and concentrate on the others.

The ice-creams are delicious and unusual. They are made from a whipped meringue and whipped cream mixture, so the volume is there before they are frozen. This means that they do not need any re-whisking, either by hand or in a machine, so that too saves time and energy. Another job that needn't be done. However, the ice-creams do contain raw egg, so do be aware when serving to the very young, the elderly or to pregnant ladies. Most eggs nowadays are stamped with a lion which is proof that the hen has been injected against salmonella. But, as with most things, there is often no guarantee.

You can go to town serving cold desserts, and I love decorating the plates. My icing sugar sifter works well, especially over the chocolate terrine, and I always have a spray of berries or currants if the dessert is fruit based. A good tip when serving ice-cream is to scoop it out into balls in advance and place back in the freezer, covered with clingfilm. This saves time, but also makes the ultimate serving much easier. Just remember to remove from the freezer 10 or so minutes in advance so that they come to eating temperature and texture.

A final thought. If you are serving two cold desserts, make sure they are quite different: one rich, gooey and calorific, the other something like a fruit salad or a sorbet. People can choose what they like – one or the other, or indeed both!

Double Chocolate Terrine **V**

Walnut Praline Parfait **V**

Quite the Best Summer Pudding **V**

Hazelnut Meringue Roulade with Passion-lemon Coulis **V**

Homemade Lemon Curd **V**

Divine Lemon Pots **V**

White Chocolate Mousses **V**

Lavender Crème Caramel **V**

Lemon Balm Ice-cream **V**

Melon Sorbet **V**

Orange Curd Ice-cream with Passionfruit and Orange **V**

Five-fruit Salad **V**

For more dessert ideas, see:

Hot Puddings section (see page 146)

Home Baking Section (see page 204)

Mincemeat Bread and Butter Pudding (see page 230)

Brandy Ice-cream (see page 232)

Frangipane Mince Pies (see page 232)

Apple Mincemeat Alaska (see page 239)

Double chocolate terrine ^{V}

Serve in thinnish slices as it is very naughty! Make the terrine 1 day ahead so that it's really firm.

Serves 10–12

WHITE CHOCOLATE LAYER	DARK CHOCOLATE LAYERS
200g (7 oz) white chocolate (Lindt Excellence)	350g (12 oz) dark chocolate (Bournville)
200ml (7 fl oz) double cream	450ml (¾ pint) double cream
	2 egg yolks
	2 tablespoons brandy

Line a 900g (2lb) loaf tin with clingfilm.

1 For the white chocolate layer, break into a bowl with the double cream and carefully melt together over a pan of hot water. Don't let the chocolate become too hot or it will go grainy; it should be slightly hotter than lukewarm. Stir until smooth. Leave to cool.

2 For the dark chocolate layers, break into a food processor and process to a fine powder. Boil half of the cream and pour in. Process until smooth then add the egg yolks and brandy. Mix until blended. Whisk the remaining cream in a bowl to soft peaks and fold into the dark chocolate mixture in a bowl. Pour some of this mixture to reach one-third of the way up the lined tin then transfer to the freezer for about 1 hour, until set. When just set, pour in the white chocolate and freeze for about 2 hours until set.

3 Spoon the remaining dark chocolate on top of the white mixture, cover and put back into the freezer for about 6 hours until firm or simply leave in the fridge overnight to set.

4 To serve, you may want to freeze the terrine for about 30 minutes, which makes cutting easier. Remove the clingfilm. Serve in slices (it helps to cut the slices with a hot knife).

cook now, eat later

TO PREPARE AHEAD This can be made up to 2 days ahead. Make completely and turn out, leaving the clingfilm intact. Peel off and decorate before serving straight from the fridge.

TO FREEZE Once set, turn out, wrap in a second layer of clingfilm and freeze for up to 1 month. Thaw for about 6 hours.

TO 'COOK' IN THE AGA Melt the chocolates in separate bowls on a tea-towel at the back of the Aga several hours ahead.

Walnut praline parfait ^V

A very easy and delicious dessert, generously given to me by Vicky, a close neighbour. Just take it out of the freezer about 10 minutes before serving – what could be easier!

Serves 8

4 eggs, separated	PRALINE
100g (4 oz) caster sugar	100g (4 oz) caster sugar
300ml (½ pint) pouring double cream	6 tablespoons water
1 teaspoon vanilla extract	100g (4 oz) walnut pieces

You will need 8 ramekins.

1 To make the praline, dissolve the sugar and water in a small saucepan (not non-stick), stirring until all the sugar is dissolved. Turn up the heat, discard the spoon, and boil until a light caramel colour. Stir in the walnuts and pour on to non-stick paper for the praline to set. Once the praline is cold, chop up into small pieces (about the size of a sultana).

2 Whisk the egg whites in a mixer, or with an electric hand whisk on maximum speed until stiff. Gradually add the sugar 1 teaspoon at a time until well incorporated and the mixture is stiff and glossy. Fold in the egg yolks.

3 Whisk the cream with the vanilla extract until just thick. Fold into the egg mixture, along with most of the chopped praline (reserve a little for garnish).

4 Pour into 8 ramekins, cover with clingfilm and freeze for a minimum of 12 hours.

5 Remove the parfait from the freezer about 10 minutes before serving, and top with the reserved walnut praline.

cook now, eat later

TO PREPARE AHEAD AND FREEZE Prepare and freeze up to 1 month before. In which case, forget the reserved praline, and simply sprinkle with icing sugar and some fresh mint.

TO COOK IN THE AGA Dissolve the sugar for the praline on the Simmering Plate, discard the spoon, then transfer to the Boiling Plate, and boil until a light caramel colour.

Quite the best summer pudding ^V

This summer pudding is all fruit and very little bread. I make it fairly shallow in a straight-sided soufflé dish or glass dish. The shallowness means that even though there is much more fruit than bread, the pudding doesn't collapse when turned out. There will be fruit left so serve it with the pudding, which should be really well chilled.

Serves 8

350g (12 oz) blackberries	350g (12 oz) caster sugar
350g (12 oz) blackcurrants	225g (8 oz) raspberries
350g (12 oz) redcurrants	8 slices thin sliced bread, crusts removed
1 small punnet, about 150g (5 oz) blueberries, if available	pouring cream to serve

You will need a 1.1 litre (2 pint) soufflé dish or straight-sided dish, 15 × 8cm (6 × 3 in).

1 Measure all the fruits except the raspberries into a pan with a tablespoon of water. Add the sugar and bring to the boil, then gently simmer until the fruits are just tender. Cool a little, then add the raspberries.

2 Cut the bread to shapes to fit the base and sides of the dish to about 5cm (2 in) up the side. Dip the bread into the juice first then line the dish, putting the fruit-soaked side nearest the dish. Fill the dish just under half full with some of the fruit, then put a layer of bread over the fruit. Add more fruit on top and finally the last slices of bread, spooning a little of the juice over the bread at the top. You should have about 200ml (7 fl oz) of fruit left over to serve with the pudding. Put a small plate on top, press down lightly, then cover with clingfilm and refrigerate overnight.

3 Turn out into a shallow dish a little larger than the summer pudding so that the juices are caught. I serve it with extra reserved fruit and pouring cream.

cook now, eat later

TO PREPARE AND COOK AHEAD Make up to 2 days ahead and keep in the fridge.

TO FREEZE Cover and freeze at the end of step 2. Thaw overnight at room temperature. The pudding will be quite soft after freezing.

TO COOK IN THE AGA Bring the fruits to the boil on the Boiling Plate, cover and transfer to the Simmering Oven for about 15 minutes or until the fruits are just tender.

Hazelnut meringue roulade with passion-lemon coulis ∨

A meringue roulade with the wonderful addition of hazelnuts. The coulis is stunning! You can make lemon curd with the egg yolks left over from the meringue.

Makes 8–10 slices

5 egg whites	COULIS
275g (10 oz) caster sugar	6 tablespoons lemon curd
50g (2 oz) shelled hazelnuts, roughly chopped	2 passionfruit
300ml (½ pint) double cream, whipped	GARNISH
	8 Cape gooseberries

Preheat the oven to 200°C/400°F/Gas 6. Line a 33 × 23cm (13 × 9 in) Swiss roll tin with greased non-stick baking paper, securing the corners with metal paperclips.

1 Whisk the egg whites in an electric mixer on full speed until very stiff. Gradually add the sugar, 1 teaspoon at a time, and still at high speed, whisk well between each addition. Whisk until very, very stiff and all the sugar had been included. Mix in two-thirds of the hazelnuts.

2 Spread the meringue mixture into the prepared tin and sprinkle the remaining hazelnuts evenly over the top. Bake in the preheated oven for about 12 minutes or until just coloured pale golden. Lower the oven temperature to 160°C/325°F/Gas 3 and continue baking for a further 20 minutes until firm to the touch.

3 Remove the meringue from the oven and turn, hazelnut side down, on to a sheet of non-stick baking paper. Remove the paper and paperclips from the base of the cooked meringue and allow to cool for about 10 minutes.

4 When cooled, spread the whipped cream over the meringue. Start to roll from the long end, fairly tightly, until rolled up like a Swiss roll. Wrap in non-stick paper and chill before serving.

5 To make the coulis, mix the lemon curd with the scooped-out seeds and juice from the passionfruit.

6 Serve the coulis alongside a slice of roulade. Garnish with a Cape gooseberry on each plate.

recipe continued overleaf

cook now, eat later

TO PREPARE AND COOK AHEAD The roulade can be made 24 hours before it is needed. Complete to the end of step 4 and keep in the fridge. The coulis can also be made up to 24 hours ahead (this time will also allow the passionfruit seeds to soften slightly).

TO FREEZE Wrap the roulade in foil at the end of step 4 and freeze for up to 2 months. Thaw the roulade for about 8 hours in the fridge.

TO COOK IN THE AGA Cook the meringue on the grid shelf on the floor of the Roasting Oven with the cold sheet on the second set of runners for about 8–10 minutes until pale golden brown. Transfer to the Simmering Oven for about 15 minutes until firm to the touch.

Homemade lemon curd

A wonderful way of using up egg yolks, having made meringues.

Makes 3 small jars

100g (4 oz) butter	grated zest and juice 3 lemons
225g (8 oz) caster sugar	5 egg yolks or 3 beaten eggs

1 Measure butter and sugar into a bowl. Stand over a pan of simmering water and sir occasionally until butter has melted. Stir lemon zest and juice and egg yolks (or eggs) into butter mixture. Cook for about 25 minutes until curd thickens, stirring occasionally. Do not allow to get too hot.

2 Remove from heat and pour into warm, clean jars.

cook now, eat later

TO PREPARE AND COOK AHEAD Keep in fridge for up to 3 months.

TO FREEZE Not suitable.

TO COOK IN THE AGA Cook in Simmering Oven for about 40 mins, stirring occasionally.

Divine lemon pots ^V

Probably the easiest dessert you will ever make — and so delicious too! It came my way from a dear friend Di. Four of us play tennis every Monday and so often swap recipes and ideas over coffee! It has become a firm favourite ever since. You don't need to add the raspberries, and the brandy can be left out too, but we prefer it with!

Serves 8

600ml (1 pint) pouring double cream	16 fresh raspberries
150g (5 oz) caster sugar	3 tablespoons brandy
finely grated zest and juice of 3 lemons	

You will need 8 small coffee cups, wine glasses or tiny ramekins.

1 Heat the cream, sugar and lemon zest in a wide-based pan over a low heat until at simmering point. Stir continuously for about 3 minutes.

2 Remove from the heat and allow to cool slightly (until lukewarm).

3 Mix the lemon juice and brandy with the cooled cream and sugar, and stir.

4 Pour the lemon cream into the cups. Transfer to the fridge to set for a minimum of 2 hours. Arrange 2 raspberries on top of each pot when the cream has set.

cook now, eat later

TO PREPARE AND COOK AHEAD These can be made up to 24 hours before serving, and kept in the fridge.

TO FREEZE Not suitable.

White chocolate mousses V

Really fast to make and memorable to eat.

Makes 8

BASE	WHITE CHOCOLATE MOUSSE
40g (1½ oz) plain Bournville chocolate	1 × 200g bar Continental white chocolate, broken into small pieces
75g (3 oz) Hobnob biscuits (without chocolate coating), coarsely crushed	200ml (7 fl oz) double cream, lightly whipped
225g (8 oz) strawberries, thinly sliced	200ml (7 fl oz) full-fat crème fraîche
fresh mint sprigs	

You will need eight 7cm (2 ¾ in) metal rings. Place on a baking sheet lined with non-stick baking paper.

1 Break the plain chocolate into a medium-sized bowl and melt over a pan of gently simmering water. Do not allow the chocolate to become too hot. Add the biscuits to the warm melted chocolate, stir to mix, then using the back of a metal spoon press into the bottom of the metal rings. Allow to set in the fridge.

2 For the mousse, break the white chocolate into a bowl and carefully melt over a pan of hot water. (Do not allow the chocolate to get too hot or it will become grainy; it should be slightly hotter than lukewarm.) Stir until smooth. Set aside to cool a little to firm up. Stir into the whipped cream and add the crème fraîche. Carefully mix until smooth.

3 Neatly arrange the strawberry slices up the sides of the rings and spoon the mousse mixture on to the individual biscuit bases. Gently level the tops. Chill until firm. Transfer to a plate, remove from the rings and decorate with mint.

cook now, eat later

TO PREPARE AHEAD Make up to 12 hours ahead, cover and keep in their rings in the fridge.

TO FREEZE Not suitable.

TO 'COOK' IN THE AGA Melt the chocolates in separate bowls on a tea-towel at the back of the Aga several hours ahead.

TIP If you haven't any metal rings, use small empty chopped tomato or baked bean cans. Take off the top and base with a can opener and wash thoroughly.

Orange curd ice-cream with passionfruit and orange ^V

There are some delicious flavours here. When buying ready-made curds, check the labels to see that the contents are just butter, sugar and eggs, and no E numbers.

Serves 8–10

4 eggs, separated
100g (4 oz) caster sugar
300ml (½ pint) double cream, lightly
   whipped
finely grated zest of 1 medium orange
6 tablespoons luxury orange curd
fresh mint leaves to decorate

PASSIONFRUIT AND ORANGE
1–1½ oranges per person
¼ passionfruit per person

1 Place the egg yolks in a small bowl and whisk until well blended. Using an electric hand whisk, whisk the egg whites until stiff, then whisk in the sugar 1 teaspoon at a time until stiff and glossy.

2 Fold the cream into the egg yolks, with the orange zest and curd. Mix in 1 spoonful of egg white and carefully fold in the remaining egg white.

3 Turn the ice-cream into a 1.4 litre (2½ pint) plastic container, cover and freeze overnight.

4 Segment the oranges. Cut each passionfruit in half, and scoop out the pulp. Mix together.

5 Serve the tangy fruit mixture with the orange curd ice-cream, and decorate with mint.

cook now, eat later

> **TO PREPARE AHEAD AND FREEZE** Prepare and freeze the ice-cream for up to 1 month. Prepare the oranges and passionfruit, cover and keep in the fridge for up to 24 hours. Remove the ice-cream from the freezer 5–10 minutes before serving and leave to stand at room temperature.

Clockwise from top left: Lemon Balm Ice-cream; Melon Sorbet;
Orange Curd Ice-cream with Passionfruit and Orange

COOKING FOR A CROWD

When cooking for a large number, you need to get down to planning as soon as you can. Think carefully about what sort of party it will be. If people are to stand to eat, they need something that can be cut with a fork alone. If you offer something like gammon, they'll need a knife and fork, and will have to sit down. Is it to be a buffet party, with cold foods and salads laid out on a table for everyone to help themselves, or will you be offering something hot, which you help them to? Ask for help and tell your helper a certain dish will serve 8 or 10, perhaps even indicating portion sizes on the dish itself.

When still at the planning stages, consider who your guests are and at what time of day the party is to be held. If they've had a long time standing and chatting, and it's a long time since breakfast or lunch, they'll probably be hungry and eat a lot – this is particularly true of younger guests! But if it's a lunch or supper party at the end of the Christmas holiday, nobody will be interested in eating too much . . .

When planning a cold buffet party, the gammon will look very impressive (and you can cook it 6 days ahead!). The *Cockatrice* (page 196) will astound everyone and, although it's complicated to assemble initially, it can be done in advance. It's best cold, and the cooking can be done two days in advance. My carving ideas concerning fillet of beef will open your eyes to its buffet potential – no more grey, unappetising slices lying limply on the plate. And never over-do the salad choice either. Stick to a couple only, rather than overwhelming your guests with potential flavours and texture. If serving a pie such as the steak and mushroom one on page 200, do so in a shallow dish so that everyone gets a bit of the crispy potato topping.

Once you have decided on the type of party and on what you plan to cook, you can order ingredients well in advance, cook, chill and freeze (if appropriate). Everything in this chapter can be prepared in advance.

Three Bean, Tomato and Asparagus Salad **V**

Herb and Parmesan Soft Rolls **V**

Peppadew and Cheddar Scone Bake **V**

Glazed Apple Gammon

Salmon and Fennel Fish Pie

Reggiori Pasta Bake with Tuna and Two Cheeses

Chilled Gazpacho Chicken

Cockatrice

The Perfect Whole Roast Fillet of Beef with Thyme

Steak and Mushroom Pie with Dauphinoise Potato Topping

Lancashire Lamb Shanks

For other ideas, see:

Any of the recipes in the other sections,
and simply double the ingredients.

Three bean, tomato and asparagus salad ^V

This can be made ahead completely as the beans can marinate in the dressing and the tomatoes will not lose too much liquid. Serve on a stylish platter for your buffet table.

Serves 10–12

1 × 400g can lentils	225g (8 oz) asparagus tips
1 × 400g can flageolet beans	10 tomatoes, skinned and sliced
1 × 400g can black-eyed beans	1 tablespoon balsamic vinegar and
4 spring onions, sliced on the diagonal	2 tablespoons olive oil, mixed
6 tablespoons good salad dressing	a handful of freshly snipped chives and
salt and freshly ground black pepper	torn basil leaves

1 Drain and rinse the lentils and beans. Pat dry on kitchen paper, then mix together in a bowl. Stir in the spring onions, salad dressing and salt and pepper. Arrange along the base of a thin flat dish.

2 Blanch the asparagus tips in boiling salted water for about 2–3 minutes until just tender, drain and refresh in cold water. Dry on kitchen paper.

3 Arrange the tomato slices over the beans, overlapping. Arrange the asparagus tips in a herringbone shape along the centre of the tomatoes.

4 Season with salt and pepper, then drizzle the balsamic vinegar and oil mixture over the whole dish. Sprinkle over the chives and basil, and serve.

cook now, eat later

TO PREPARE AHEAD Make completely to the end of step 3 up to some 12 hours ahead.

TO FREEZE Not suitable.

Herb and Parmesan soft rolls ^V

This is a quick and easy way of making rolls. You can make them by hand or use a dough hook which will save time and effort. This recipe can also be used to make two small 450g (1 lb) loaves, but naturally they will take a little longer to bake.

Makes 20 rolls

500g (1 lb 2 oz) strong white flour, plus extra for kneading

4 tablespoons olive oil, plus extra for glazing

350ml (12 fl oz) warm water

3 teaspoons salt

1 × 7g packet fast-action yeast

50g (2 oz) Parmesan, freshly grated, plus extra for sprinkling

25g (1 oz) fresh chives, snipped

a good handful of fresh basil leaves, chopped

a good handful of fresh parsley, chopped

sunflower seeds

1 Measure the flour, oil, water, salt and yeast into the mixer and mix using the dough hook for 5–8 minutes – the mixture will look quite wet – or mix by hand. Put into a large oiled bowl covered with clingfilm. Place in the fridge overnight.

2 The next day take the dough out of the fridge. It should have doubled in bulk. Leave the dough on one side for 1 hour to bring back to room temperature, then knock back by kneading in the mixer or on a floured surface for 5 minutes by hand.

3 Add the cheese and herbs and continue to knead until they are well incorporated. Divide the dough into 20 pieces and roll into balls. Place these close together on a greased baking sheet, and cover with an oiled plastic bag. (A cleaners' suit plastic bag is ideal – just tie a knot in the plastic where the hanger hole is.) Leave to prove in a warm place for about 30 minutes until the rolls have doubled in size.

Meanwhile, preheat the oven to 200°C/400°F/Gas 6.

4 Lightly glaze the rolls with oil and sprinkle with sunflower seeds and Parmesan. Bake in the preheated oven for about 20–25 minutes until well risen, golden and the rolls sound hollow when tapped on the base. Best served warm.

cook now, eat later

TO PREPARE AND COOK AHEAD Complete step 1 the day before. Or the rolls can be baked the day before they are needed and then refreshed in a moderate oven at 180°C/350°F/Gas 4 for 15 minutes when required.

TO FREEZE Cool the cooked rolls completely, pack into a plastic bag and freeze for up to 3 months. Thaw at room temperature. Refresh in a moderate oven as above for about 10–15 minutes.

TO COOK IN THE AGA Bake the rolls for about 20–30 minutes on the grid shelf on the floor of the Roasting Oven. Check after 15 minutes. Remove the grid shelf and put the baking sheet directly on the floor of the Roasting Oven to brown the bases.

Peppadew and Cheddar scone bake V

Lovely for a lunch box or with soup or salad. Serve with butter or cream cheese. These can be cut into more than 12 pieces if you want a smaller slice.

Makes 12 squares

450g (1 lb) self-raising flour	225g (8 oz) mature Cheddar, grated
4 teaspoons baking powder	100g (4 oz) peppadew bell peppers,
1 teaspoon salt	drained and finely sliced
½ teaspoon mustard powder	2 eggs
freshly ground black pepper	milk
100g (4 oz) butter, at room temperature	

Lightly grease a 30 × 23cm (12 × 9 in) traybake tin or roasting tin. Preheat the oven to 230°C/450°F/Gas 8.

1 Measure the flour, baking powder, salt and mustard powder into a large bowl and add a little black pepper. Add the butter and rub into the flour using the fingertips until the mixture resembles fine breadcrumbs. Stir in the cheese and peppers.

2 Break the eggs into a measuring jug, beat together, and make up to 300ml (½ pint) with milk. Add to the flour mixture, mixing to form a soft dough.

3 Knead the dough quickly and lightly until smooth, then roll out on a lightly floured work surface to an oblong to fit the roasting tin. Mark into 12 squares and brush the top with a little milk.

4 Bake in the preheated oven for about 20 minutes until the scone is well risen and golden. Turn out on to a wire rack to cool. Break apart to serve.

cook now, eat later

TO PREPARE AND COOK AHEAD Bake up to 24 hours in advance, then reheat and refresh in the tin in a moderate oven at 180°C/350°F/Gas 4 for about 10 minutes.

TO FREEZE Allow the baked scone to cool completely, then pack into a strong polythene bag and freeze for up to 3 months. Thaw at room temperature and reheat and refresh in a moderate oven as above to serve.

TO COOK IN THE AGA Slide the traybake tin on to the grid shelf on the floor of the Roasting Oven for about 15 minutes or until a perfect golden brown. Slide the plain cold sheet on to the second set of runners and bake for a further 5–10 minutes until firm and shrinking away from the sides of the tin.

Glazed apple gammon

There is nothing like home-cooked ham for Christmas or for a buffet. For a change we have cooked this one in apple juice which complements the meat perfectly (use the sort you buy in cartons). If you buy gammon from the butcher, it may be a special cure and need soaking before cooking — ask his advice. Supermarket gammons do not usually need soaking.

Serves 20 at least

4kg (9 lb) half gammon, unsmoked	2 generous tablespoons redcurrant jelly
2 litres (3½ pints) apple juice	1 tablespoon Dijon mustard

1 Place the gammon in a large pan just big enough to hold it, and cover with the apple juice. Bring to the boil over a high heat. Turn the heat down to simmer, cover and cook very gently for about 4 hours (55 minutes per kg, 25 minutes per lb) until tender. I advise using a meat thermometer (the thermometer should read 75°C when done), but put it in at the end as it must not be submerged in liquid. To test for doneness without a thermometer, pierce the gammon with a skewer — it should feel tender as the skewer goes into the meat.

2 Allow the meat to cool in the liquid. Remove from the pan, and place on a piece of foil in a small roasting tin. Gently remove the skin, leaving the fat on top. Melt the redcurrant jelly, stir in the mustard and spread evenly over the fat of the ham. Score the glaze diagonally with a sharp knife, cutting through the fat. Wrap the lean meat in foil.

3 Glaze and brown under the grill or glaze in a preheated oven at 220°C/425°F/Gas 7 until golden brown and crisp – about 15 minutes.

4 If serving cold, chill in the fridge for 12 hours or so before carving.

cook now, eat later

TO PREPARE AND COOK AHEAD The completed gammon can be made up to 6 days ahead and kept in the fridge.

TO FREEZE Not suitable.

TO COOK IN THE AGA Bring to the boil on the Boiling Plate, cover and transfer to the Simmering Oven for about 4–5 hours (depending on your Simmering Oven) until tender. Glaze at step 3 in a roasting tin on the highest set of runners in the Roasting Oven until golden brown and crisp.

Salmon and fennel fish pie

This is a fish pie for a very special occasion. Adding ricotta cheese to the mashed potato lightens the texture and gives an interesting flavour.

Serves 12

700g (1½ lb) fresh fennel bulbs
300ml (½ pint) dry white wine
about 800ml (1½ pints) hot milk
100g (4 oz) butter
100g (4 oz) plain flour
salt and freshly ground black pepper
1.4kg (3 lb) salmon fillet, skinned and cut
   into 1cm (½ in) pieces
2 tablespoons chopped fresh dill

8 eggs, hard boiled and cut into eighths

TOPPING
1.6kg (3½ lb) King Edward potatoes
   (weight before peeling), peeled and
   cut into large chunks
500g (1 lb 2 oz) ricotta cheese
about 8 tablespoons milk
100g (4 oz) Parmesan, freshly grated

You will need one shallow ovenproof dish, capacity 3 litres (5 pints), about 35 × 25 × 5cm (14 × 10 × 2 in), or two shallow ovenproof dishes, capacity 1.4 litres (2½ pints), about 28 × 23 × 5cm (11 × 9 × 2 in). Preheat the oven to 200°C/400°F/Gas 6.

1 For the topping, cook the potatoes in boiling salted water until tender. Drain well.

2 Whilst the potatoes are cooking, cut the fennel bulbs in half from top to bottom, and remove and discard the core. Cut into quarters and then slice in horseshoe shapes. Put into a small pan with the wine, and simmer until the fennel is soft, about 10 minutes. Drain the fennel, reserving the liquid, and make up to 1.1 litres (2 pints) with the milk.

3 Next make the sauce. Melt the butter in a medium pan, add the flour and stir to mix. Gradually add the milk and fennel liquid, stirring continuously, and allowing to thicken. Season well, bring to the boil, and simmer for a few minutes, then add the salmon pieces and cook for a further few minutes. Stir in the fennel and dill, check the seasoning, and spread into the dish or dishes. Scatter the eggs over the sauce. Press down gently into the fish mixture.

4 Mash the potatoes until smooth. Stir in the ricotta cheese, adding enough milk to give a creamy texture, and plenty of salt and pepper. Spoon over the fish and sauce, spreading the potatoes right to the edge of the dish. Sprinkle with the Parmesan.

5 Bake in the preheated oven for about 30–35 minutes until cooked through, brown and crisp and piping hot. If using two dishes, change the dishes around half-way through the cooking time if necessary.

recipe continued overleaf

cook now, eat later

TO PREPARE AND COOK AHEAD Prepare the pie(s) to the end of step 4. Cover with clingfilm and keep in the fridge for up to 1 day. Follow step 5 to cook – it will take about 10 minutes longer cooking from cold.

TO FREEZE Not suitable.

TO COOK IN THE AGA Bake the assembled dish on the grid shelf on the floor of the Roasting Oven for about 30 minutes until the potato is crisp and golden and the pie is piping hot.

Reggiori pasta bake with tuna and two cheeses

Rigatoni is large tube-shaped pasta, ideal for use in a baked pasta dish such as this one.

Serves 12

1 large onion, coarsely chopped	a little paprika
350g (12 oz) dried rigatoni pasta	
2 × 400g cans tuna in brine, drained well	CHEESE SAUCE
2–3 tablespoons capers, drained and roughly chopped	100g (4 oz) butter
2 tablespoons snipped fresh chives	100g (4 oz) plain flour
4 large tomatoes, about 400g (14 oz), skinned and roughly chopped	1.1 litres (2 pints) milk
salt and freshly ground black pepper	2 teaspoons Dijon mustard
150ml (¼ pint) double cream	4 tablespoons chopped fresh parsley
	50g (2 oz) mozzarella cheese, grated
	50g (2 oz) Gruyère cheese, grated

Preheat the oven to 200°C/400°F/Gas 6. You will need two 28 × 23 × 5 cm (11 × 9 × 2 in) shallow ovenproof dishes, lightly buttered.

▎ Cook the onion in boiling salted water with the pasta until al dente. Drain and refresh with cold water until completely cold. Drain well then divide between the prepared ovenproof dishes.

2 Next make the sauce. Melt the butter in a large pan, take off the heat and stir in the flour. Gradually add the milk, stirring continuously, and bring to the boil. Season with salt, pepper and mustard, and simmer for 2 minutes. Add the parsley and half of each cheese. Stir to mix.

3 Mix the tuna, capers, chives and tomatoes in a bowl and season well with salt and pepper. Spoon over the pasta in the dishes, spreading the tuna out evenly. Pour the cheese sauce over the tuna mixture in the dishes.

4 Next pour over the cream and scatter over the remaining cheeses. Sprinkle with paprika.

5 Bake in the preheated oven for about 30 minutes until the top is golden and bubbling.

cook now, eat later

TO PREPARE AND COOK AHEAD Prepare to the end of step 3 up to 24 hours ahead. Cool, cover and keep in the fridge. Complete steps 4 and 5 to serve.

TO FREEZE Add 150ml (¼ pint) more milk to the cheese sauce if you wish to freeze the pasta bake after step 3. Don't pour over the cream or scatter with the cheese yet. Cover and freeze for up to 1 month. Thaw overnight in the fridge. Complete step 4 and heat as in step 5, increasing the time to about 40 minutes, or until piping hot.

TO COOK IN THE AGA Bake the assembled dish on the grid shelf on the floor of the Roasting Oven for about 25 minutes.

Chilled gazpacho chicken

Gazpacho is an old favourite cold soup for summer. I have combined the raw ingredients with cooked chicken to make an up-to-date Coronation chicken. You can of course use cooked turkey instead of the chicken.

Serves 12 (as part of a buffet)

2 medium chickens, cooked (yielding about 900g/2 lb flesh)

200ml (7 fl oz) 'light' low-calorie mayonnaise

200ml (7 fl oz) full-fat crème fraîche

4 tablespoons sun-dried tomato paste

18–20 peppadew bell peppers, drained and thinly sliced

2 garlic cloves, crushed

12 spring onions, white part only, thinly sliced

4 teaspoons balsamic vinegar

4 tablespoons chopped fresh basil, plus a handful of leaves to garnish

salt and freshly ground black pepper

GARNISH SALAD

2 small cucumbers, peeled, seeded and cut into pieces

500g (1 lb 2 oz) cherry tomatoes, cut in half

100g (4 oz) black olives (the best are in olive oil from the deli counter)

chopped fresh parsley

a little French dressing

1 Cut the chicken into neat bite-sized pieces, removing all the skin and bone.

2 Mix the mayonnaise and crème fraîche with the tomato paste, peppers and garlic. Fold in the chicken pieces and spring onions, then taste and season carefully with the balsamic vinegar, basil, salt and pepper.

3 Spoon out on to a flat serving dish and garnish with the dressed salad and basil leaves.

cook now, eat later

TO PREPARE AHEAD Prepare the chicken to the end of step 2, cover and keep in the fridge for up to 24 hours ahead. The garnish salad can be prepared up to 12 hours ahead, but do not dress. Spoon the chicken on to a flat serving dish and garnish with the salad and fresh basil.

TO FREEZE Not suitable.

TIP Peppadew peppers are small bell peppers from South Africa, found in jars in good delis and supermarkets. They are available hot or mild, and we like the mild ones best. Once opened, keep in the fridge, and use them in salads, pasta, stuffed with cream cheese, and in any of the recipes here (see pages 188 and 252).

Cockatrice

Three birds in one. The earliest mention of this idea I have found is in Elizabeth Raffald's English Housekeeper *in 1769. It was called 'Yorkshire Goose Pie' and consisted of many boned birds, one inside the other, a goose, then a turkey, then 2 ducks and then a few woodcocks. It was then covered with pastry and baked for 4 hours and then 2 pounds of butter were poured on top of the pie. It was served cold. Ours is a healthier, simpler version!*

This variation of Cockatrice was given to me recently in Guernsey by Steve Halstead, the senior chef lecturer at the catering college. He and some of his students gave me great support when I was demonstrating on the island. I've never had my herbs chopped at such speed!

Ask your butcher to bone the birds for you and give him plenty of notice; you can freeze them ahead. Thaw thoroughly before stuffing and assembling the Cockatrice. Ask him for the bones and giblets for gravy. There is no need to tunnel-bone the birds — cutting down the backbone makes it easier to assemble. If you wish to freeze the raw completed Cockatrice, use fresh boned birds, not frozen. Cockatrice can be served hot with port gravy, but we prefer it cold. If you can't get frozen chestnuts, use 100g (4 oz) dried chestnuts soaked overnight.

Serves 20

1 × 5.5kg (12 lb) turkey, boned and last drumstick bone left in
1 × 2.5kg (5½ lb) duck, boned
1 × 1kg (2¼ lb) chicken, boned
salt and freshly ground black pepper
plenty of butter, softened

STUFFING
2 onions, finely chopped
50g (2 oz) butter
175g (6 oz) streaky bacon, snipped
225g (8 oz) frozen chestnuts, thawed and roughly chopped
50g (2 oz) fresh white breadcrumbs
2 tablespoons dried sage

225g (8 oz) spinach, chopped, or 450g (1lb) frozen chopped spinach, thawed and drained
450g (1 lb) good pork sausages, skinned
1 egg

PORT GRAVY (IF SERVING HOT)
50g (2 oz) butter
1 onion, roughly chopped
50g (2 oz) plain flour
150ml (¼ pint) red wine or port
1.1 litres (2 pints) stock made from the chicken and turkey bones
1–2 tablespoons cranberry or redcurrant jelly

Preheat the oven to 220°C/425°F/Gas 7.

❙ First make the stuffing. Cook the onion in the butter until soft, without colouring. Add the bacon and chestnuts. Stir from time to time until lightly browned. Remove from the heat and add the breadcrumbs, sage and spinach. Allow to become cold. Mix in the sausages, egg and 1 teaspoon each of salt and pepper. I find it easiest to mix using my hands.

2 Lay each bird, breast side down, on the work surface. Trim the excess fat from the duck, and season well inside each bird.

3 Take a quarter of the stuffing and stuff the chicken, then re-shape roughly. Spread another quarter of stuffing liberally over the duck and put the stuffed chicken inside the duck. Wrap up neatly in an approximation of its former shape. There is no need to sew up either of the birds. Repeat with the remaining stuffing and turkey. You can sew up the Cockatrice but I find it much easier to use skewers. Shape it to look as much like a plain turkey as possible. Tie 3 lengths of string around the bird and 1 from end to end. Also tie the legs together.

4 Butter the turkey breast well, and put a meat thermometer into the centre of the Cockatrice. Wrap loosely in foil and roast in the preheated oven for about 1 hour. Lower the temperature to 160°C/325°F/Gas 3, and cook for a further 2 hours until the thermometer reads 75°C. You can also test with a skewer: the juices should run clear. It is essential not to undercook. Increase the oven temperature to 220°C/425°F/Gas 7, open the foil and brown the breasts of the bird, about 10 minutes. Rest or cool if serving cold.

5 For the gravy if serving hot, heat the butter, add the onion and cook slowly until lightly browned. Stir in the flour, scraping well on the bottom of the pan, then pour in the red wine or port and allow to reduce slightly. Slowly stir in the stock and add cranberry or redcurrant jelly to taste. Bring to the boil and season.

6 To serve the Cockatrice hot, allow to rest with a covering of foil – this will make carving easier and allow the juices to settle. Carve straight across the bird taking slices from the end first. Sadly it does not hold together very well when served hot but it tastes delicious.

7 To serve the Cockatrice cold, roast 2 days ahead, cool and refrigerate. To carve, cut in half across the middle then cut the back end in half again. Cut fairly thick slices from these two quarters to start with. Serve with *Scarlet Confit* (see page 227).

cook now, eat later

TO **PREPARE AND COOK AHEAD** Stuff and wrap the raw bird in foil in the fridge 1 day ahead. Roast and cook completely 2 days ahead, cool well and refrigerate.

TO **FREEZE** Freeze for up to 1 month raw. Thaw for 2 days in the fridge.

TO **COOK IN THE AGA** At step 4 roast in the Roasting Oven on the grid shelf on the floor for about 1 hour then transfer to the Simmering Oven for about 1½ hours until done (longer if you have a slow Simmering Oven).

The perfect whole roast fillet of beef with thyme

Cold rare roast fillet of beef is sheer luxury for a special occasion. So often a beautifully cooked fillet is carved too early, arranged on a platter and in an hour or so after exposing the cut surface to the air the meat turns grey – so disappointing. However, a very easy solution is to carve the cold fillet up to 6 hours ahead and then reassemble it back into a roast fillet shape and to tightly wrap it in clingfilm. Then just arrange it on the platter immediately before serving. Ask the butcher to tie the joint neatly so that it keeps its round shape during roasting.

If you like very hot horseradish, use hot horseradish instead of the creamed. For me, life is too short to grate fresh horseradish!

Serves 8–12
(depending upon whether you are serving other cold meats as well)

1.5kg (3 lb) fillet of beef, cut from the thick end	HORSERADISH SAUCE
12 large sprigs of fresh thyme	generous ½ x 185g jar horseradish cream
3 garlic cloves, crushed	3 tablespoons whipped or thick cream
3 tablespoons olive oil	
salt and freshly ground black pepper	

1 First marinate the beef for 24 hours. Put the fillet into a strong polythene bag with the thyme, garlic, oil and pepper. Keep in the fridge in the marinade for up to 24 hours.

Preheat the oven to 220°C/425°F/Gas 7.

2 Heat a non-stick frying pan until hot. Lift the thyme out of the marinade and put to one side. Seal the beef on all sides using the oil from the marinade in the hot frying pan. When gloriously brown lift out on to foil in a roasting tin and sprinkle with salt.

3 Roast in the preheated oven for 30 minutes (10 minutes per 450g/1 lb). The internal temperature should be 60°C for rare if you use a meat thermometer. (Not quite so rare, 62–63°C.)

4 Leave to become completely cold before carving (see introduction).

5 A nice garnish is to fry the fresh thyme, which makes it bright green, or just decorate with parsley. Serve with the horseradish sauce made from a mixture of the horseradish cream and whipped cream.

recipe continued overleaf

cook now, eat later

Steak and mushroom pie with dauphinoise potato topping

Few people have a large enough dish for 12, so you can make this in two 30 × 23 × 6cm (12 × 9 × 2½ in) if preferred. It is important to part-cook the potatoes ahead, otherwise they will go black.

Serves 12

2kg (4½ lb) good stewing steak, cut into 2.5cm (1 in) cubes
sunflower oil
4 large onions, roughly chopped
700g (1½ lb) small open (dark-gilled) mushrooms, sliced
a good 4 tablespoons plain flour
about 1.1 litres (2 pints) beef stock
2 tablespoons Worcestershire sauce
salt and freshly ground black pepper
a little gravy browning (optional)

DAUPHINOISE POTATO TOPPING
2.2kg (4¾ lb) old potatoes, peeled
about 100g (4 oz) butter, melted
150g (5 oz) Cheddar, grated

You will need a shallow ovenproof dish, about 38 × 28 × 8cm (15 × 11 × 3 in).

1 Brown the meat, in batches, in a little oil in a large frying pan, over a high heat. Remove from the pan.

2 Add the onion to the pan, fry for a couple of minutes, then lower the heat and simmer for about 10 minutes until soft. Add the mushrooms and flour. Cook, stirring, for 1 minute then add the stock, Worcestershire sauce, seasoning and a little gravy browning if liked. Bring to the boil, and allow to thicken, stirring until smooth.

3 Return the meat to the pan, bring back to the boil, then cover and simmer very gently for about 2 hours, until the meat is tender. (Or cook in the oven preheated to 160°C/325°F/Gas 3 until tender, perhaps nearer 3 hours.)

4 For the topping, cook the potatoes in boiling salted water until just tender. Cool a little, then slice thickly and toss in the melted butter.

Preheat the oven to 200°C/400°F/Gas 6.

5 Spoon the meat into . Layer the potatoes on top, seasoning well in between the layers. Top with the cheese. Cook in the preheated oven for about 30 minutes until the cheese is bubbling and golden and the meat is hot through.

cook now, eat later

TO PREPARE AND COOK AHEAD Prepare and cook the steak to the end of step 3. Cool, cover and keep in the fridge for up to 2 days. Cook the potatoes, slice and toss in the melted butter earlier in the day. Assemble the pie as in step 5, then reheat until piping hot at the same temperature, allowing a little longer from cold.

TO FREEZE Freeze the cooked meat base only for up to 3 months. Thaw overnight, then assemble the pie, and reheat as above, allowing a little longer from cold.

TO COOK IN THE AGA Fry the onions and meat and make the gravy on the Boiling Plate. Transfer to the Simmering Oven, covered, for about 2½–3 hours or until tender. Continue steps 4 and 5. When the potato topping is added, cook at the top of the Roasting Oven for about 30 minutes until golden brown.

Lancashire lamb shanks

It is wonderful that we can buy lamb shanks so easily in supermarkets. They are often cooked with a tomato and red wine based sauce, so I have developed this recipe using a light sauce with white wine and herbs. Do cook the shanks really well until the meat falls off the bone. If you like crisper vegetables, add them to the stew for the last hour only.

Serves 12

12 lamb shanks, about 350g (12 oz) each in weight	2 large onions, peeled and cut into eighths
salt and freshly ground black pepper	2 large carrots, peeled, cut into 2.5cm (1 in) batons
1 tablespoon sunflower oil	2 butternut squashes, total weight 900g (2 lb), peeled and cut into 2.5cm (1 in) slices
100g (4 oz) butter	
175g (6 oz) plain flour	
1.1 litres (2 pints) white wine	masses of chopped fresh parsley
750ml (1¼ pints) good chicken or lamb stock	

1 Heat a large frying pan. Season the lamb shanks with salt and pepper. Brown the shanks in the oil and butter on each side until golden brown (you will need to do this in batches). Transfer the shanks to a deep stewpan large enough to hold all 12 of them (and the vegetables).

2 Make the sauce in the original frying pan. Add the flour to the fat left in the pan. Mix together off the heat, return to the heat, and gradually add the wine and stock. Bring to the boil, stirring all the time, until the sauce boils and becomes thickish and smooth in consistency. Season with salt and pepper and pour this sauce over the shanks in the casserole.

3 Bring the sauce and shanks back to the boil, cover with the lid and simmer for about 1½ hours.

4 Add the vegetables, pushing them down so they are covered with the sauce, and bring back to the boil. Cover with the lid and simmer for a further 1–1½ hours or until the vegetables are just tender and the meat is falling off the bone. Check the seasoning. (If preferred, cook in a preheated slow oven at 160°C/325°F/Gas 3, following the same instructions as above.)

5 Stir in the parsley and serve with *Leek Mash* (see page 106).

cook now, eat later

TO PREPARE AND COOK AHEAD The whole casserole can be made up to 2 days before and kept covered in the fridge. Add the vegetables for slightly less time, as they will continue to cook when the casserole is reheated. Reheat gently so as not to break up the vegetables.

TO FREEZE Not suitable.

TO COOK IN THE AGA Brown the shanks on the Boiling Plate until golden brown. Cook from step 3 covered in the Simmering Oven for about 2–2½ hours or until the shanks are tender.

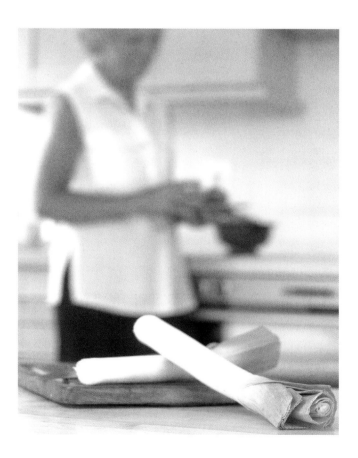

HOME BAKING

As you know, home baking is one of my passions, and I love creating new cakes, biscuits and traybakes. One of the principal advantages of home baking is that most cakes can be frozen: you can cool them, wrap them well and freeze as soon as possible after baking, and they will emerge as good as new after a couple of months. Cakes might need icing after defrosting (many icings look best when fresh), and scones and muffins will need to be oven-refreshed, but the basic work has all been done well in advance.

Baking needs to be a little more precise than many other aspects of cookery. For instance, it really is essential to weigh everything correctly. Usually people weigh 'heavy', so you should check your scales against a packet of sugar or butter. The right size of tin is essential as well: have a ruler or tape measure handy to check the width and depth of each tin. So often people say a particular sponge recipe hasn't worked, and it's turned out that they've used the wrong tin. It makes a huge difference.

And ingredients are very important too. Use natural sugars if you can, as they contain no dyes. All the recipes call for large eggs, and organic are best. Be careful with baking powder: if you use even fractionally too much, the cake will rise up then fall down again! Fats are a contentious issue now. The method I use for mixing cakes before baking is the all-in-one method. All the ingredients are put into the bowl then beaten together with a hand whisk until smooth. I once used baking margarines with an 80 per cent fat content, and these, like butter, would be slightly softened before mixing. However, these margarines seem to have disappeared from the market to a large extent for some reason, and I am often obliged to use spreads with a reduced fat content (70–73 per cent) instead, such as Stork Tub, Flora Original or Flora Buttery. Because of the reduced fat content, these need to be used straight from the fridge, otherwise they would be too soft and the cake mix would be too runny. Always look at the packaging: ideally you want 80 per cent fat margarine, to use at room temperature.

Ginger and Orange Cake with Mascarpone Icing V

Double Chocolate Chip Brownie Cake V

Lemon and Lime Traybake V

Banoffee Traybake V

Apricot and Brandy Cake V

Chocolate and Rum Cake V

Apricot and Walnut Breakfast Muffins V

Sultana Spice Traybake V

Orange Chocolate Shortbread Biscuits V

Fresh Raspberry Scones V

Mega Chocolate Cookies V

Apple and Lemon Drop Scones V

For more baking ideas, see:

Herb and Parmesan Soft Rolls (see page 186)

Peppadew and Cheddar Scone Bake (see page 188)

Frangipane Mince Pies (see page 232)

Classic Victorian Christmas Cake (see page 234)

Christmas Chocolate Log (see page 236)

Ginger and orange cake with mascarpone icing ^v

A delicious and light cake, best kept in the fridge because of the icing. This cake is a true favourite with all who work with me!

Cuts into 8–10 wedges

225g (8 oz) self-raising flour	4 eggs
2 level teaspoons baking powder	5–6 bulbs stem ginger in syrup, coarsely
225g (8 oz) baking margarine or butter,	chopped, plus syrup
at room temperature	finely grated zest of 1 orange
225g (8 oz) caster sugar	1 × 250g tub mascarpone cheese

Preheat the oven to 180°C/350°F/Gas 4. Base-line two 20cm (8 in) deep sandwich tins with non-stick paper, and grease well.

1 Measure the flour, baking powder, margarine or butter, sugar, eggs, 3–4 bulbs of the ginger and the grated orange zest into a large mixing bowl. Using an electric hand mixer, mix well until thoroughly blended. Divide the mixture evenly between the prepared tins and level out.

2 Bake in the centre of the preheated oven for 20–25 minutes until golden brown and shrinking away from the sides of the tin. Leave to cool for a few moments then turn out.

3 For the filling/icing, beat the mascarpone with 2 tablespoons of the ginger syrup. When the cakes are completely cold, sandwich with half of this mixture. Spread the remainder on top of the cake and sprinkle over the remaining coarsely chopped ginger.

cook now, eat later

TO PREPARE AND COOK AHEAD Make the cakes and store in an airtight container for up to 3 days before filling and icing. Make the filling/icing when you need it.

TO FREEZE The cakes freeze well un-iced. Wrap and freeze for up to 3 months. Thaw for about 4 hours at room temperature, then fill and ice.

TO COOK IN THE AGA **2-oven Aga:** Bake on the grid shelf on the floor of the Roasting Oven with the cold shelf on the second set of runners for about 25 minutes. Turn half-way through baking.

4-oven Aga: Bake on the grid shelf on the floor of the Baking Oven for 25 minutes, sliding in the cold shelf on the second set of runners only if the cakes become too dark.

Double chocolate chip brownie cake ^V

A quick and easy chocolate cake. Making two loaves allows you to freeze one for another day.

Makes 2 loaves

100g (4 oz) ground almonds	2 level teaspoons baking powder
225g (8 oz) baking margarine or butter, at room temperature	150g (5 oz) white chocolate buttons
175g (6 oz) self-raising flour	ICING
225g (8 oz) light muscovado sugar	200g (7 oz) dark chocolate (Bournville)
50g (2 oz) cocoa powder	50g (2 oz) butter
5 eggs	25g (1 oz) white chocolate buttons

Grease and line two 450g (1 lb) loaf tins (top measurement 17 × 11cm/6½ × 4 in). Preheat the oven to 180°C/350°F/Gas 4.

1 Measure all the ingredients for the cake, except the white buttons, into a bowl and mix until smooth. Fold in the white chocolate buttons and pour into the tins. Level the surface.

2 Bake in the middle of the preheated oven for about 1 hour or until well risen, firm to the touch and shrinking away from the sides of the tin. Allow the cakes to cool on a wire rack.

3 For the icing, put the dark chocolate and butter into a bowl. Place over a pan of simmering water to melt. Stir, leave for 2 minutes, then spread over the top of the cakes. Dot the white chocolate buttons on to the warm chocolate icing.

cook now, eat later

TO PREPARE AND COOK AHEAD Bake and ice, up to 3 days ahead. The icing, though, is better made nearer the time of serving.

TO FREEZE Cool, pack and freeze the un-iced cakes for up to 3 months. Thaw at room temperature for about 4 hours. Ice as directed in the recipe.

TO COOK IN THE AGA **2-oven Aga:** Place the tins on the grill rack in the large roasting tin. Slide on to the lowest set of runners in the Roasting Oven with the cold sheet on the second set of runners. Bake for about 30 minutes until the cakes are well risen and set. Carefully transfer to the Simmering Oven for about 25 minutes.

4-oven Aga: Place the tins on the grill rack in the large roasting tin. Slide on to the lowest set of runners in the Baking Oven for about 35–45 minutes. Check half-way through cooking: if too brown, slide the cold sheet on to the second set of runners.

For the icing, melt chocolate and butter in Simmering Oven for about 10 minutes.

Apricot and brandy cake ᵛ

A beautifully moist, rich cake: ice it for Christmas, or serve plain at any time of year. Make the cake at least 2 weeks ahead so that it is not crumbly. You can feed it with more brandy if you like once it is cooked. Just turn the cake upside down and spoon over a few tablespoons of brandy.

We've also tried this in a 23cm (9 in) round cake tin. It makes a shallower cake, taking about 4¼–4½ hours' cooking time.

Makes 1 × 20cm (8 in) cake

225g (8 oz) ready-to-eat dried apricots,
    chopped
90ml (3½ fl oz) brandy
225g (8 oz) butter, at room temperature
225g (8 oz) light muscovado sugar
225g (8 oz) plain flour
5 eggs
225g (8 oz) currants

450g (1 lb) sultanas
350g (12 oz) glacé cherries, rinsed, dried
    and quartered

TO DECORATE
apricot jam for glaze
ready-to-eat dried apricots and
    glacé fruits

1 Soak the chopped apricots in the brandy overnight.

Grease and line a 20cm (8 in) deep round cake tin with a double layer of greased greaseproof paper. Preheat the oven to 140°C/275°F/Gas 1.

2 Cream the butter and sugar together in a very large mixing bowl, then add the remaining ingredients and continue to mix until well blended.

3 Spoon the mixture into the prepared tin and spread out evenly with the back of a spoon. Cover the top of the cake loosely with a double layer of greaseproof paper.

4 Bake in the preheated oven for about 5 hours or until the cake is a pale golden colour, feels firm to the touch and a skewer inserted into the centre comes out clean. Allow the cake to cool in the tin.

5 Turn out the cake. Glaze with apricot jam. Slice whole apricots in half horizontally and cut any large glacé fruits into slivers if rather thick. Arrange in groups over the top of the cake and glaze again.

recipe continued overleaf

Orange chocolate shortbread biscuits ∨

A variation on an old classic, and very easy to make. The chocolate becomes crisp and crunchy.

Makes 20 biscuits

175g (6 oz) butter, softened	75g (3 oz) cornflour or semolina
75g (3 oz) caster sugar	1 × 85g bar Terry's chocolate orange,
175g (6 oz) plain flour	chopped into small pieces

Preheat the oven to 190°C/375°F/Gas 5. Lightly grease two baking trays.

1 Measure the butter and sugar into a food processor and process until soft. Add the flour and cornflour or semolina and process until beginning to form coarse breadcrumbs. Scrape down the sides, remove the blade and stir in the chocolate pieces.

2 Shape the mixture into 20 even-sized balls and put on to the prepared baking trays. Flatten each ball with a fork. Bake in the preheated oven for about 15–20 minutes until the edges of the biscuits are golden. Allow to cool for a few minutes then transfer to a wire rack until cold.

cook now, eat later

TO PREPARE AND COOK AHEAD Bake, cool and store the biscuits in an airtight container for up to 1 week.

TO FREEZE Pack the cooked biscuits into a rigid freezer-proof container and freeze for up to 2 months. Thaw at room temperature for 1–2 hours.

TO COOK IN THE AGA 2-oven Aga: Place the baking sheet on the floor of the Roasting Oven for about 4 minutes. Take out of the oven, put the grid shelf on the floor and return the biscuits to the grid shelf. Cook for a further 4 minutes until just pale golden at the edges. Do watch very carefully, if necessary sliding the cold sheet on the second set of runners above the biscuits to prevent further browning. Transfer to the Simmering Oven for a further 30–35 minutes until the biscuits are cooked through.

4-oven Aga: Bake on the floor of the Baking Oven for 5 minutes. Take out of the oven, put the grid shelf on the floor and return the biscuits to the grid shelf. Cook for a further 10 minutes until just pale golden at the edges. Watch carefully, if necessary sliding the cold sheet on the second set of runners above the biscuits to prevent further browning. Transfer to the Simmering Oven for a further 30–35 minutes until the biscuits are cooked through.

Clockwise from left: Mega Chocolate Cookies; Frangipane Mince Pies; Orange Chocolate Shortbread Biscuits

Fresh raspberry scones ^V

Fresh blueberries can replace the raspberries if wished, but we prefer the raspberries! The scone dough is very deep to cut out once layered with the raspberries, so flour the cutter well between each cutting to prevent the dough sticking.

The large scone made from the trimmings is perfect sliced for the family.

Makes about 12 small scones

450g (1 lb) self-raising flour	2 eggs
4 teaspoons baking powder	milk
100g (4 oz) butter, softened	about 100g (4 oz) fresh raspberries
50g (2 oz) caster sugar	

Lightly grease 2 baking trays. Preheat the oven to 220°C/425°F/Gas 7.

1 Measure the flour and baking powder into a large bowl. Add the butter and rub in with the fingertips until the mixture resembles fine breadcrumbs. Stir in the sugar.

2 Break the eggs into a measuring jug, then make up to 300ml (½ pint) with milk. Stir the egg and milk mixture into the flour – you may not need it all – and mix to a soft but not sticky dough.

3 Turn out on to a lightly floured work surface, knead lightly and then roll out to a rectangle about 2cm (¾ in) thick. Cut the rectangle of dough into 2 equal pieces.

4 Scatter the fresh raspberries evenly over 1 piece of dough. Top with the second rectangle of dough. Cut into as many rounds as possible with a fluted 5cm (2 in) cutter, and place them on the prepared baking trays. Gently push the trimmings together to form 1 large scone, and score the top with a sharp knife. Brush the tops of the scones with a little extra milk, or any egg and milk left in the jug.

5 Bake in the preheated oven for about 15 minutes or until the scones are well risen and a pale golden brown. (The large scone will need about a further 5 minutes.) Lift on to a wire rack to cool. Eat as fresh as possible.

cook now, eat later

TO PREPARE AND COOK AHEAD Best eaten on the day of making. If you must, store in the fridge for 1 day once cooked. To serve, refresh in a preheated oven at 180°C/350°F/Gas 4 for about 10 minutes.

TO FREEZE These freeze extremely well. Freeze the cooled scones in plastic bags for up to 6 months. Thaw in the plastic bags for 2–3 hours at room temperature, and reheat to serve as above.

TO COOK IN THE AGA Cook on the grid shelf on the lowest set of runners of the Roasting Oven for about 10–15 minutes.

CHRISTMAS AT HOME

All my Christmases have been at home in recent years, but I well remember when we used to take everything – the turkey, stuffing, vegetables, all prepared in advance – over to Granny's on Christmas Eve, ready to be cooked the next day. It was all a matter of meticulous organisation, and that still applies today.

Order your turkey or goose well in advance. If choosing a frozen turkey, the fresh frozen are better than the water-cooled. Defrost thoroughly in a cool place – *not* the fridge, and *not* a freezing garage! The stuffings can be made and frozen well ahead, as can things like mince pies, ice-cream and cakes. And of course, if you've made a Christmas pudding yourself, that will be ready several months in advance.

For the day itself, the turkey can be stuffed (breast end only) some hours before cooking, so long as it is in the fridge. Make a stock from the giblets the day before. If making the chestnut stuffing, look out for those wonderful frozen chestnuts, which appear just before Christmas in the best supermarkets. If you can't get hold of them, use the dried, but remember to buy half the weight asked for in the recipe – they plump up after an overnight soak. You could already have breadcrumbs for the stuffing in the freezer, but make sure you have pure white for the bread sauce. You can prepare the vegetables the day before – peeling, trimming and chopping – and if you're offering a root vegetable purée, that could be happily in the fridge awaiting its reheating. Part-roast your potatoes and parsnips ready for a quick blast in the oven once the turkey is resting.

The recipes here are traditional, but most have a twist, something you might like to try – and that your family might appreciate – just as a change on Christmas Day. The puddings in particular are different. You could try the ice-cream instead of brandy butter with your Christmas pudding (and it could be made with rum instead). All can be prepared ahead, making for a relaxed and enjoyable day for all – especially the cook!

Traditional Roast Turkey

Scarlet Confit

Apricot and Chestnut Stuffing

Lemon and Thyme Pork Stuffing

Mincemeat Bread and Butter Pudding

Frangipane Mince Pies

Brandy Ice-cream

Classic Victorian Christmas Cake

Christmas Chocolate Log

Apple Mincemeat Alaska

For more Christmas ideas, see:

Spicy Turkey Fajitas (see page 140)

Turkey Salad with Avocado, Bacon and Pesto Dressing (see page 141)

Glazed Apple Gammon (see page 189)

Cockatrice (see page 196)

Apricot and Brandy Cake (see page 210)

Traditional roast turkey

I use a meat thermometer when cooking turkey – it helps to judge when the turkey is done. Cook it to 75°–80°C rather than the 90°C suggested on the thermometer gauge.

Serves about 20

1 × 7.5kg (17 lb) oven-ready turkey
butter, softened
lemon, thinly sliced

sprigs of fresh thyme
onion

Preheat the oven to 220°C/425°F/Gas 7.

1 Loosen the skin over the breast of the turkey by slipping your fingers between the flesh and skin, leaving the skin attached at the neck end. Spread softened butter over the top of the breast under the skin, holding the skin up. Slip in lemon slices and thyme, under the skin.

2 Stuff the breast end of the turkey with *Lemon and Thyme Pork Stuffing* (see page 229). Secure the loose skin with fine skewers. Fill the body cavity with any lemon trimmings, herbs and large pieces of onion. Tie the legs with string to give a neat shape. Lightly butter the skin of the bird.

3 Weigh the turkey and calculate the cooking time, allowing 15 minutes per 450g (1 lb). Arrange 2 large sheets of foil across a large roasting tin. Place the turkey on top and insert a meat thermometer into the thickest part of the thigh. (When cooked it will register 75°–80°C.) Fold the sheets of foil loosely over the turkey, leaving a large air gap between the turkey and the foil.

4 Cook the turkey in the preheated oven for about 30 minutes. Reduce the oven temperature to 160°C/325°F/Gas 3 and cook for 30 minutes short of the cooking time, basting from time to time.

5 Remove the foil 30 minutes before the end of cooking time and increase heat to 220°C/425°F/Gas 7 to crisp the skin.

6 If not using a thermometer, pierce the thickest part of the thigh with a small sharp knife. If the juices are clear, then the turkey is done; if they are still tinged with pink, then cook for a little longer. Cover turkey and leave to stand for 30 minutes before carving.

7 Drain off the liquid from the tin, skim off the fat and keep the stock for gravy.

8 Serve with bacon rolls, gravy, sausages, bread sauce, *Scarlet Confit* (see page 227) and *Apricot and Chestnut Stuffing* (see page 228).

recipe continued overleaf

cook now, eat later

TO PREPARE AHEAD Prepare to the end of step 3 up to 12 hours before. Cover and chill until ready to cook.

TO FREEZE The raw stuffings can be frozen for up to 1 month in advance.

TO COOK IN THE AGA **Slow roasting:** Place on the grid shelf on the floor of the Simmering Oven. If the turkey is over 8.1kg (18 lb), or if your Simmering Oven is on the cool side, start off in the Roasting Oven uncovered for 30 minutes, then cover with foil and transfer to the Simmering Oven (see chart below).

3.6–4.5kg (8–10 lb) turkey, about 10 hours

5–7.25kg (11–16 lb) turkey, about 12 hours (overnight)

7.5–10kg (17–22 lb) turkey, about 14 hours (overnight)

To brown, when the bird is done, put uncovered into the Roasting Oven for about 15 minutes.

Fast roasting: Cook in the roasting tin lightly covered with foil on the grid shelf on the floor of the Roasting Oven.

3.6–4.5kg (8–10 lb) turkey, about 1¾–2 hours

5–7.25kg (11–16 lb) turkey, about 2½ hours

7.5–10kg (17–22 lb) turkey, about 3 hours

Baste the bird from time to time. Remove the foil 30 minutes before the end of cooking time to crisp the skin.

TIP Do not put a meat stuffing into the cavity of a bird as this is not safe. Put in only flavouring, vegetables and herbs.

Scarlet confit

Gently reheat to serve with hot game casseroles and roast turkey or game birds.

Serves 20

450g (1 lb) fresh or frozen cranberries	50ml (2 fl oz) cider vinegar
225g (8 oz) granulated sugar	a large pinch of ground allspice
finely grated zest and juice of 1 orange	a large pinch of ground cinnamon
50ml (2 fl oz) port	

1 Measure all the ingredients into a shallow pan.

2 Bring to the boil and simmer gently for about 10–15 minutes, stirring from time to time. Don't worry if it looks a bit runny as it thickens when it cools.

cook now, eat later

TO PREPARE AND COOK AHEAD Cook and keep covered in the fridge for up to 1 month.

TO FREEZE Cool quickly, pack and freeze for up to 3 months. Leave at room temperature to defrost.

TO COOK IN THE AGA Cook uncovered in the Simmering Oven for about 1 hour.

Apricot and chestnut stuffing

A really good stuffing to serve with turkey, chicken or goose.

Serves 6

225g (8 oz) ready-to-eat dried apricots
600ml (1 pint) water
1 large onion, coarsely chopped
225g (8 oz) white breadcrumbs
75g (3 oz) butter

225g (8 oz) frozen chestnuts, thawed
  and roughly chopped
a generous bunch of fresh parsley,
  chopped
salt and freshly ground black pepper

You will need a shallow ovenproof dish, about 20 × 28 × 5cm (8 × 11 × 2 in).

Preheat the oven to 190°C/375°F/Gas 5.

1 Chop the apricots into small pieces, the size of raisins.

2 Measure the water into a pan, add the onion and apricot pieces, and boil for 5 minutes. Drain well.

3 Put the breadcrumbs into a large bowl. Melt the butter in a pan and pour half of it on to the breadcrumbs.

4 Add the chestnuts to the remaining melted butter and brown lightly. Mix together with the apricots, onion, parsley and breadcrumbs. Season well and taste.

5 Turn into a buttered, ovenproof dish and bake for about 25–30 minutes until crisp.

cook now, eat later

TO PREPARE AND COOK AHEAD Prepare to the end of step 4. Cover and keep in the fridge for up to 1 day before cooking. Cook as above but for a little longer.

TO FREEZE Freeze at the end of step 4 for about 1 month. Defrost and reheat to serve as above until piping hot.

TO COOK IN THE AGA Slide the dish on to the floor of the Roasting Oven for about 25–30 minutes until crisp.

Lemon and thyme pork stuffing

This is a favourite family recipe, served for every Christmas as long as I can remember! This is the stuffing for the breast end of the turkey: do not put a meat stuffing in the body cavity of a bird.

Sufficient to stuff a 7.2–8.1 (16–18 lb) turkey in the breast end

40g (1½ oz) butter
1 large onion, chopped
700g (1½ lb) pork sausagemeat
150g (5 oz) fresh white breadcrumbs
finely grated zest and juice of
   1 large lemon

salt and freshly ground black pepper
3 tablespoons chopped fresh parsley
leaves from 6 sprigs of fresh thyme,
   or 1 level teaspoon dried thyme

1 Melt the butter in a saucepan, add the onion and cook gently until soft, about 10 minutes.

2 Stir in the remaining ingredients and mix well together.

cook now, eat later

TO PREPARE AND COOK AHEAD Make the day before, cover and keep in the fridge.

TO FREEZE The stuffing can be made and frozen for up to 3 months so long as the pork sausagemeat has not been previously frozen. Leave at room temperature to defrost.

TO COOK IN THE AGA Cook the onion in the Simmering Oven until soft.

Mincemeat bread and butter pudding

This is wonderful at any time of the year, not just at Christmas! It is essential to make it in a shallow dish so that you get maximum crunchy top. It rises like a soufflé, so serve at once straight from the oven.

Serves 6–8

50g (2 oz) ready-to-eat dried apricots	3 large eggs
2 tablespoons brandy or rum	150ml (¼ pint) double cream
12 thin slices white bread, buttered	1 teaspoon vanilla extract
1 × 450g jar luxury mincemeat	300ml (½ pint) milk
50g (2 oz) caster sugar	1 tablespoon demerara sugar

Well butter a 28cm (11 in) fairly shallow, round, china ovenproof dish. Preheat the oven to 180°C/350°F/Gas 4.

1 Snip the apricots into smallish pieces and soak in the brandy or rum whilst making the pudding.

2 Make sandwiches of the bread using the mincemeat, but don't fill right to the edges because they are trimmed off. Cut off the crusts and cut each sandwich diagonally into four. Arrange the sandwich triangles across the dish, slightly overlapping.

3 Beat together the caster sugar, eggs, cream and vanilla extract. Stir in the milk.

4 Scatter the apricots over the bread. Gradually pour over the cream mixture, making sure all the bread is coated. Leave the pudding to stand for 30–60 minutes. (This allows the bread to absorb the liquid so it becomes light and crisp during cooking.)

5 Sprinkle the demerara sugar over the top of the pudding, and bake in the preheated oven for about 40 minutes until well risen, crisp and golden. Serve warm with crème fraîche or cream.

cook now, eat later

TO PREPARE AHEAD Complete to the end of step 4 up to 12 hours ahead, cover with clingfilm and leave in the fridge. Continue with step 5.

TO FREEZE Not suitable.

TO COOK IN THE AGA Bake on the grid shelf on the floor of the Roasting Oven, with the cold sheet on the second set of runners, for about 25 minutes.

Frangipane mince pies

A new variation on an old favourite. If you want to make a large tart you can use the exact quantity below to fill a 23cm (9 in) loose-bottomed flan tin which will take about 25 minutes in the preheated oven.

Makes 24

PASTRY
225g (8 oz) plain flour
100g (4 oz) butter, cut into cubes
25g (1 oz) icing sugar
1 egg, beaten

FRANGIPANE
100g (4 oz) softened butter
100g (4 oz) caster sugar
2 large eggs
100g (4 oz) ground almonds

15g (½ oz) plain flour
½ teaspoon almond extract, or to taste

FILLING AND TOPPING
just under 1 × 410g jar mincemeat
   flavoured with about 2 tablespoons
   brandy
a few flaked almonds
apricot jam to glaze

You will need deep mince pie tins for 24 pies and a 6.5cm (2½ in) cutter.

Preheat the oven to 200°C/400°F/Gas 6.

1 To make the pastry, measure the flour, butter and icing sugar into a food processor bowl, then process until the mixture resembles breadcrumbs. Pour in the beaten egg and pulse the blade until the dough starts to form a ball. Knead lightly, wrap and chill for about 30 minutes.

2 To make the frangipane, measure the butter and sugar into the unwashed processor, and blend until soft and creamy. Scrape down the sides, add the eggs and continue to process. Don't worry if the mixture looks curdled at this stage. Add the ground almonds, flour and almond extract, and mix briefly.

3 Roll the pastry out thinly on a lightly floured work surface and line the tins. Spoon a teaspoon of mincemeat into each tartlet and top with the frangipane mixture. There is no need to spread the mixture flat as it will level out in the oven (but do not over-fill the tins). Sprinkle a few flaked almonds on top.

4 Bake in the preheated oven for about 15–17 minutes, watching carefully. Remove from the tins and allow to cool a little on a wire rack.

5 Dilute the apricot jam with a little lemon juice or water and bring to the boil. Brush each warm tartlet with glaze. Like traditional mince pies, these are best served warm.

TO PREPARE AND COOK AHEAD Complete to the end of step 5 up to 3 days ahead. Refresh in a moderate oven at 180°C/350°F/Gas 4 for about 8–10 minutes.

TO FREEZE Freeze the mince pies at the end of step 5. Thaw at room temperature for 2–3 hours. Warm through in the oven as above.

TO COOK IN THE AGA Bake directly on the floor of the Roasting Oven for about 8 minutes to brown the pastry base. Turn round and slide on the grid shelf on the floor of the Roasting Oven for a further 6–8 minutes until well risen and golden brown. You may need the cold sheet on the second set of runners if getting too brown.

Brandy ice-cream

This ice-cream does not need a second whisking so is very quick and easy, and is very good with Christmas pudding, mince pies and tarts. It contains raw egg yolks so is not suitable for pregnant ladies or the very young or elderly.

Serves 8

4 eggs, separated	300ml (½ pint) double cream
100g (4 oz) caster sugar	2 tablespoons brandy

1 Whisk the egg whites on fast speed, using an electric hand whisk, until light and stiff. Beat in the sugar, still on a fast speed, a little at a time until a thick glossy meringue. Fold in the egg yolks.

2 Whisk the cream and brandy together until thick. Fold into the meringue mixture.

3 Freeze in a flat polythene box overnight, for at least 12 hours.

cook now, eat later

TO PREPARE AHEAD AND FREEZE Freeze for up to 1 month.

Classic Victorian Christmas cake

Remember to make time, some 3 days, for marinating the fruit in sherry. This is essential to plump up and flavour the fruit. If you cut the soaking time, there will be surplus liquid which will alter the texture of the cake. You should make this cake at least 3 weeks ahead of Christmas, for if eaten too early it is crumbly. This is not a very deep cake.

Makes 1 × 23cm (9 in) cake

175g (6 oz) raisins
350g (12 oz) glacé cherries, rinsed and
   dried thoroughly
500g (1 lb 2 oz) currants
350g (12 oz) sultanas
150ml (¼ pint) sherry
finely grated zest of 2 oranges
250g (9 oz) softened butter
250g (9 oz) light muscovado sugar
4 eggs
1 tablespoon black treacle

75g (3 oz) blanched almonds, chopped
75g (3 oz) self-raising flour
175g (6 oz) plain flour
1½ teaspoons mixed ground spice

TO FINISH AND DECORATE

medium sherry
apricot jam
glacé fruits
nuts

1 First prepare the fruit: chop the raisins with a damp knife and quarter the cherries. Put all the fruit in a container, pour over the sherry and stir in the orange zest. Cover with a lid and leave to soak for 3 days, stirring daily.

Grease and line a 23cm (9 in) deep round tin with greased greaseproof paper. Preheat the oven to 140°C/275°F/Gas 1.

2 Measure the butter, sugar, eggs, treacle and almonds into a large bowl and beat well. Add the flours and spice and mix thoroughly until blended. Stir in the soaked fruit. Spoon into the prepared cake tin and level the surface. Cover the top of the cake loosely with a double layer of greaseproof paper.

3 Bake in the centre of the preheated oven for about 5–5½ hours or until the cake feels firm to the touch and is a rich golden brown. A skewer inserted into the centre of the cake should come out clean. Leave the cake to cool in the tin.

4 When cool, pierce the cake at intervals with a fine skewer and feed with a little sherry. Wrap the completely cold cake in a double layer of greaseproof paper and again in foil and store in a cool place for up to 3 months, feeding at intervals with more sherry. (Don't remove the lining paper when storing as this helps to keep the cake moist.)

5 To decorate, brush sieved, warmed apricot jam over the top of the cake. Arrange glacé fruits and nuts over the jam and brush again with jam.

cook now, eat later

TO PREPARE AND COOK AHEAD Prepare the fruit and soak in sherry 3 days ahead. Make the cake and wrap as in step 4. Store in a cool place for up to 3 months, following step 4.

TO FREEZE Freeze for up to 3 months, then defrost at room temperature.

TO COOK IN THE AGA Baking the cake slowly in the Simmering Oven gives excellent results. Don't bake overnight, as it could be overbaked. I find it best to mix the cake and put it into the tin the day before, then bake it starting first thing in the morning in the Simmering Oven. Choose a day when you are at home and can keep an eye on it. In my Aga it takes 5½ hours. In a converted Aga or old Aga with a slower Simmering Oven, I find it best to start it off in the Roasting Oven on the grid shelf on the floor with the cold shelf on the second set of runners for about 30 minutes or until just pale golden, then transfer to the Simmering Oven until done. Consult your original Aga book.

Christmas chocolate log

An easy Yule log, with a delicious filling and icing. The apricot jam helps the icing to stick to the cake, and is delicious too. You don't need to wait until Christmas, though the cake can be made at any time of the year for a special occasion.

Serves 10–12

CHOCOLATE SPONGE	CHOCOLATE ICING AND TOPPING
4 large eggs	275g (10 oz) Bournville chocolate, in
100g (4 oz) caster sugar	small pieces
65g (2½ oz) self-raising flour	450ml (¾ pint) double cream
40g (1½ oz) cocoa powder	4 tablespoons apricot jam
	icing sugar for dusting

Preheat the oven to 200°C/400°F/Gas 6. Grease and line a 33 × 23cm (13 × 9 in) Swiss roll tin with non-stick paper, securing the corners with metal paperclips.

1 For the sponge, whisk the eggs and sugar using an electric hand whisk in a large bowl until the mixture is pale in colour, light and frothy. Sift the flour and cocoa powder into the bowl and carefully cut and fold together, using a metal spoon, until all the cocoa and flour is incorporated into the egg mixture. (Be careful not to beat any of the air out of the mixture.)

2 Pour into the lined tin and spread out into the corners. Bake in the middle of the preheated oven for about 8–10 minutes until pale golden and the sides are shrinking away from the edge of the tin.

3 Place a piece of greaseproof paper bigger than the Swiss roll on the work surface. Invert the cake on to the paper and remove (and count!) the paperclips and bottom lining piece of paper.

4 Trim the edges of the cake with a sharp knife and make a score mark 2.5cm (1 in) in along the longer edge. Roll up (from the longer edge) using the paper, rolling with the paper inside. Set aside to cool.

5 While the cake is cooling, make the icing. Melt the chocolate and 300ml (½ pint) of the cream in a bowl over a pan of simmering water until completely melted (be careful not to overheat). Put into the fridge to cool and firm up (this icing needs to be very thick for piping). Whip the remaining cream.

recipe continued overleaf

BITS AND BOBS
TO GO WITH DRINKS

Preparing what I call 'bits and bobs' for drinks parties is generally considered to be very labour-intensive. And so it is: everything is smaller, so shaping, cutting and putting toppings and garnishes on bases is much more intricate and detailed. This takes time as well, but all the recipes here can be prepared in advance, so it won't seem too much of a chore. The different stages may have to be brought together and/or cooked at the last minute, but the bulk of the work is out of the way. All you will have to do on the day is make things look pretty on platters.

Dips are very useful, and the two here can be made a bit in advance, and can be used with crudités or spread on crostini or pitta breads. The crostini themselves are a huge life-saver to me: store them in the freezer in plastic boxes with kitchen paper in between the layers. They're immediately to hand, take no time to defrost, and are handy for any topping. The Roquefort and pear crostini were the hit of last Christmas in our household (although I have to admit I used Stilton, as we had so much left over). The smoked salmon canapés may sound fiddly, but they're not at all, due to the crafty way we put them together (and in advance!). But the best canapés of the lot are the soufflé croûtons which are so simple and delicious, and can be baked straight from the freezer.

When planning a drinks party, have it clear in your head – and make it clear to your guests too! – exactly what it is you are offering. What time of day will it be, will people be hungry? You're not meant to be offering them a meal, just something to accompany the drinks. Bite-sized canapés that are full of flavour are the order of the day usually, and I work on about 5 per person. But if you think people might like something more substantial, you could make more canapés in general, or make some of the dishes here a little larger – the toad in the hole, for instance, baked in mince-pie tins.

Tiny New Potatoes with Dill Herrings

Roquefort and Pear Crostini **V**

Sweet Pepper and Herb Dip **V**

Scrumptious Smoked Salmon Canapés

Miniature Bangers and Mash

Wonderful Soufflé Croûtons **V**

Mustard and Parmesan Cheese Straws **V**

Cocktail Toad in the Hole

Home-made Garlic Herb Cheese **V**

Peppadew and Chèvre Crostini **V**

For more canapé ideas, see:

Garlic-stuffed Grilled Mussels (see page 22)

Crab Cakes with Mild Chilli Sauce (see page 30)

Spinach and Feta Frittata (see page 110)

Bean Bangers (see page 111)

Herb Falafels (see page 119)

Onion, Apple and Stilton Little Quiches (see page 120)

Frangipane Mince Pies (see page 232)

Tiny new potatoes with dill herrings

An unusual canapé to go with drinks. Buy the smallest new potatoes you can buy. Dill herrings come in a jar (found in the chilled section of any good supermarket with pâtés and smoked salmon) and are very versatile.

Makes 20

10 very small new potatoes, skin on	3 tablespoons crème fraîche
1 × 275g jar herrings in dill marinade	a few sprigs of fresh dill

1 Cook the potatoes in boiling salted water until tender, about 8–10 minutes. Drain, refresh in cold water (to stop the cooking), leave to cool and dry.

2 Slice the potatoes in half lengthways. Slice a very thin layer from the rounded end of each potato half (opposite the sliced side), so they will sit flat on a plate.

3 Drain the herrings from the marinade and slice into 1cm (½ in) pieces (or pieces about half the size of the potato). Spoon a tiny blob of crème fraîche on top of each potato and place a piece of herring on top, with a sprig of dill to garnish.

cook now, eat later

TO PREPARE AND COOK AHEAD These can be completely made up to 12 hours ahead, and kept in the fridge.

TO FREEZE Not suitable.

From back to front: Mustard and Parmesan Cheese Straws;
Wonderful Soufflé Croûtons; Miniature Bangers and Mash;
Tiny New Potatoes with Dill Herrings; Roquefort and Pear Crostini

Roquefort and pear crostini ᵛ

Unusual for a small drinks party, too time-consuming to do for 100! These must be served warm. They even reheat well once made, but they look their best straight from the oven.

Makes 25

1 × 400g can pears	**CROSTINI**
100g (4 oz) Roquefort cheese	1 small thin, long baguette
paprika	olive oil
chopped fresh chives	salt and freshly ground black pepper

Preheat the grill to the highest setting.

1 First make the crostini. Thinly slice the baguette, brush both sides with oil, season and place on a small baking sheet which will fit under the grill or line the grill pan with foil.

2 To cook the crostini, toast under the grill for about 2–3 minutes each side until pale golden brown and crisp. Watch them carefully. Cool on a wire rack.

3 Drain and slice the pears into thickish pieces about the thickness of a digestive biscuit in a shape just smaller than the crostini.

4 The next process is messy! Either spread a little Roquefort on each crostini then top with pear and spread with a little more Roquefort, or first grate the Roquefort on a coarse grater then spread.

5 When ready to serve, sprinkle with paprika and place under a hot grill for about 4–5 minutes or until the cheese has melted. Sprinkle with chives.

cook now, eat later

TO PREPARE AND COOK AHEAD These can be assembled up to 12 hours ahead. Cover with clingfilm and keep in the fridge until needed. Grill to serve.

TO FREEZE The crostini can be made up to 2 months in advance and frozen. Defrost and assemble with the pears and Roquefort.

TO COOK IN THE AGA For the crostini, arrange them on a baking sheet, cook on the floor of the Roasting Oven, turning once, until golden brown, about 5 minutes. To cook when assembled, slide the baking sheet on the second set of runners in the Roasting Oven for about 4–5 minutes until pale golden and the cheese has melted on the crostini. Watch very carefully. Allow to cool for a moment then scatter with chives and serve.

Sweet pepper and herb dip ᵛ

A quick and easy dip to make for pitta bread or raw vegetables, and it can also be used as a sauce for a cold cooked chicken salad. Jars of red peppers are available in all good supermarkets or, of course, you could skin a fresh pepper and use that instead. If you do not have a food processor, chop the herbs and red pepper by hand and mix with the other ingredients.

Makes about 600g (1 lb 5 oz)

leaves from a large bunch of fresh parsley	200g (7 oz) 'light' low-calorie
leaves from a large bunch of fresh basil	mayonnaise
100g (4 oz) red pepper, from a jar	150g (5 oz) full-fat cream cheese
(½ × 225g jar)	(e.g. Philadelphia)
juice of 1 lemon	salt and freshly ground black pepper
1 tablespoon caster sugar	
1 × 200g tub full-fat Greek yogurt	

1 Process the parsley and basil until coarsely chopped in a food processor.

2 Add the red pepper, lemon juice and sugar and whizz for 30 seconds.

3 Add the yogurt, mayonnaise, cream cheese and salt and pepper. Whizz again, check the seasoning and serve.

cook now, eat later

TO PREPARE AHEAD Prepare ahead, and keep covered in the fridge for about 1 week.

TO FREEZE Not suitable.

Scrumptious smoked salmon canapés

This recipe is a wonderful way to make canapés for large numbers of people. It freezes brilliantly in the tin and really is so easy to make – saves all the individual spreading and arranging! Use good-quality slices of smoked salmon for this recipe and not trimmings.

Makes 96

300g (11 oz) full-fat cream cheese	6 slices thinly sliced Hovis bread
finely grated zest of ½ lemon	(large loaf size)
a good handful of fresh dill, chopped	400g (14 oz) smoked salmon slices
salt and freshly ground black pepper	a little black caviar or lumpfish roe
	a few fresh sprigs of dill for garnish

Line a 33 × 23cm (13 × 9 in) Swiss roll tin or flat baking sheet with clingfilm (if you wet the tin first the clingfilm will stick more easily!).

1 Mix the cream cheese, lemon zest and chopped dill together in a bowl and season with salt and pepper. Remove the crusts from the bread and carefully spread each slice with the cream cheese (right into the corners), making sure all the bread is covered.

2 Arrange the bread on the lined tray, cheese side up, so all the sides are touching (3 × 2), and gently spread the cream cheese over the joins, so it looks like one large piece of cheese-covered bread. Slice the smoked salmon into long thin strips and arrange neatly over the cream cheese so all the bread is covered. Cover with clingfilm, and chill for at least 4 hours.

3 Cut into about 96 neat, even-sized squares, and top each square with a tiny blob of caviar or lumpfish roe or a sprig of fresh dill. (It works out at 16 squares per slice of bread, but you can make them larger if you like.)

cook now, eat later

TO PREPARE AHEAD AND FREEZE Freeze the tray after step 2, covered in clingfilm, up to 1 month ahead. Remove from the freezer, leave for about 10 minutes at room temperature, and cut into squares while frozen. Leave to defrost in the fridge, then top with caviar or lumpfish roe and dill.

Miniature bangers and mash

Rather than boiling only 2 small potatoes to fill the sausages, why not boil extra and use the leftovers for supper. Don't forget to warn the guests if the sausages are very hot. When making food for a drinks party, don't forget old favourites like devils-on-horseback (prunes wrapped in bacon). If you haven't already tasted them, cocktail sausages are wonderful served with equal quantities of runny honey and mustard. Coat over the sausages while hot!

Makes 20

20 cocktail pork sausages (Marks & Spencer and some supermarkets sell them ready cooked)	salt and freshly ground black pepper
	grated Parmesan
	paprika
mashed potatoes	

1 Grill the sausages (if raw), turning once or twice until cooked and evenly brown. Allow the sausages to become completely cold as it makes it easier to make a slit down the length to form an opening.

Preheat the oven to 200°C/400°F/Gas 6.

2 Ensure that the potatoes are very well seasoned. Fill into a piping bag fitted with a plain narrow nozzle. (You can also spoon the potato into the sausage.)

3 Hold a sausage, squeezing the ends gently together, and pipe or spoon the potato into the gap.

4 Sprinkle the sausages with Parmesan and dust with paprika. Arrange on a baking tray.

5 Reheat in the preheated oven for about 10 minutes or until piping hot.

cook now, eat later

TO PREPARE AND COOK AHEAD Prepare to the end of step 4 up to 1 day before. Cover and keep in the fridge. Continue with step 5.

TO FREEZE At the end of step 4, pack the sausages in a single layer in a ridged freezer container. Freeze for up to 1 month. Thaw for about 2 hours at room temperature before reheating as in step 5 above.

TO COOK IN THE AGA Cook the sausages on non-stick paper in a roasting tin on the floor of the Roasting Oven until cooked and brown. Reheat in the Roasting Oven on the top set of runners for about 5 minutes.

Wonderful soufflé croûtons ^V

These are fantastic, so easy to make, and wonderful for nibbles to go with drinks. This batch makes about 100, so great to do for a large number of people. We were given this recipe by one of our Aga enthusiasts who is a caterer and has been to many of our Aga Workshops. We thank her hugely.

Makes about 100

75g (3 oz) full-fat cream cheese	5 × 2.5cm (1 in) slices from a white tin
150g (5 oz) butter	loaf, 2–3 days old, crusts removed
150g (5 oz) Cheddar, grated	salt and freshly ground black pepper
2 large egg whites	

Preheat the oven to 220°C/425°F/Gas 7. Line 2–3 baking sheets with non-stick baking paper or grease lightly.

1 Melt the cream cheese, butter and Cheddar in a pan over a low heat until completely melted (don't worry, the mixture looks very curdled at this stage). Whisk the egg whites until stiff, and fold carefully into the cheese mixture. Season lightly with salt and pepper.

2 Cut each slice of bread into 4 down, 5 across to give 20 × 2.5cm (1 in) cubes for each slice. Dip each cube into the soufflé mixture until completely coated and transfer to the prepared baking sheets.

3 Bake in the preheated oven for about 10 minutes until golden brown and puffed up. Turn over once and check after 6 minutes. Serve at once.

cook now, eat later

TO PREPARE AHEAD AND FREEZE Freeze the raw croûtons at the end of step 2 on the baking sheet for up to 1 month. Remove from the freezer and cook from frozen for about 5 minutes longer than the cooking time above. They freeze brilliantly.

TO COOK IN THE AGA Slide the baking sheet directly on to the floor of the Roasting Oven and bake for about 10–12 minutes, turning the croûtons over once, until golden brown and puffed up. Check after about 6 minutes as they can easily catch. Serve at once.

Mustard and Parmesan cheese straws ^V

Cheese straws which aren't too fiddly! The mustard gives a lovely dark side to the straws too.

Makes about 40 straws (or 16 long ones)

1 × 375g (13 oz) packet ready-rolled puff pastry, approx. 35.5 × 23cm (14 × 9 in)	50g (2 oz) Parmesan, grated
2–3 tablespoons Dijon mustard	salt and freshly ground black pepper
	1 large egg, beaten

Preheat the oven to 220°C/425°F/Gas 7. Lightly grease 2 baking trays or line the trays with non-stick baking paper.

1 Unroll the pastry on a floured work surface and spread mustard over the top. Sprinkle evenly with Parmesan, salt and pepper. Cover with clingfilm and, using a rolling pin, roll the cheese into the pastry for a few minutes. Remove the clingfilm.

2 Divide the pastry in 4 widthways and cut each section into 10 strips about 1cm (½ in) thick for each straw. Twist each straw and place on the prepared baking trays. For extra-long cheese straws, cut the pastry in half widthways and divide each section into 8 strips, about 2.5cm (1 in) thick.

3 Glaze with the beaten egg and bake in the preheated oven for about 8–10 minutes (12 minutes for the long ones). Check the short straws after 5 minutes, the long after 8, to make sure they are not getting too brown. When the pastry is cooked through and golden brown, remove from the baking sheet and cool on a cooling rack.

cook now, eat later

TO PREPARE AND COOK AHEAD These can be made, cooked, cooled and then packed in a covered container and kept in the larder for 2–3 days. When storing, place between kitchen paper in a sealed container – this will stop them from becoming soggy. Refresh in the oven preheated to 200°C/400°F/Gas 6 for a few minutes to regain their crispness before serving.

TO FREEZE Cook, cool and freeze for up to 2 months. Thaw for about 15 minutes at room temperature. Refresh in the oven as above before serving.

TO COOK IN THE AGA Bake on the floor of the Roasting Oven for about 8 minutes, checking after 4 minutes. If the pastries are getting too brown, slide the cold sheet on to the second set of runners. When they are a perfect colour, transfer to the Simmering Oven to dry out.

Cocktail toad in the hole

Loved by both children and grown-ups! A wonderful way of using up leftover cocktail sausages.

Makes 36 'toads'

3 dozen cocktail pork sausages	250ml (8 fl oz) milk
100g (4 oz) plain flour	vegetable oil (optional)
2 eggs	creamed horseradish, mustard or mango
1 egg yolk	chutney (optional)

Preheat the oven to 220°C/425°F/Gas 7. You will need three 12-hole cocktail size tartlet tins.

1 Grill the sausages until completely cooked and golden brown (see above, or buy them ready cooked).

2 Measure the flour into a bowl, make a well in the centre of the flour and blend in the eggs and yolk with a little of the milk. Whisk to a smooth paste. Blend in the remaining milk to make a batter, and whisk really well until smooth.

3 Add a drop of oil (or fat from the sausages) to each tartlet tin. Slide the tins into the preheated oven to heat the fat. When the fat is smoking, drop a cooked sausage into the bottom of each tin and pour over the smooth batter. Return to the oven and bake for about 12–15 minutes until the batter is risen and golden brown. Check underneath one of the 'toads': it should be golden brown.

4 Spoon a tiny amount of horseradish, mustard or mango chutney on to each sausage before serving if liked. Allow to cool slightly, but serve warm.

cook now, eat later

TO PREPARE AND COOK AHEAD The sausages can be cooked up to 3 days ahead and kept in the fridge. The completed 'toads' can be made up to 14 hours ahead and reheated in the oven at 200°C/400°F/Gas 6 for about 5 minutes until hot right through.

TO FREEZE Not suitable.

TO COOK IN THE AGA Cook the sausages on non-stick paper in a roasting tin on the floor of the Roasting Oven until cooked and brown. Heat the oil on the second set of runners in the Roasting Oven and bake the 'toads' until well risen and golden brown, about 12–15 minutes. If reheating, do so in the Roasting Oven on the grid shelf on the floor for about 5 minutes until warmed through.

Home-made garlic herb cheese ^V

This cheese is so easy and yet so delicious, and, if you grow your own herbs, it is cheap too. Parsley, basil and chives are essential, but you can omit the others if preferred, or if they are unavailable.

Makes about 400g (14 oz)

a small bunch of fresh parsley	about 350g (12 oz) rich cream cheese
3 sprigs of fresh basil	1–2 small garlic cloves, crushed
2 sprigs of fresh thyme	a little single cream
1 sprig of fresh tarragon	salt and freshly ground black pepper
a small bunch of fresh chives	

1 Take the stalks off the parsley and discard. Remove the leaves from the stems of the other herbs. Snip the chives finely.

2 Put the parsley, basil, thyme and tarragon leaves in a food processor and chop finely. Add the cheese and garlic, thin down with a little cream and season. Mix in the chives.

3 Serve on the cheese board or use for recipes. Good spread thinly on crostini.

cook now, eat later

TO PREPARE AHEAD

Prepare, cover and keep in the fridge for 2–3 days.

TO FREEZE Not suitable.

Peppadew and chèvre crostini ⱽ

Peppadew peppers can be bought in jars in good supermarkets.

Makes 20–25

about 2 tablespoons olive oil	a little double cream
I garlic clove, crushed	I × 375g jar peppadew peppers
a thin French stick/baguette	fresh basil leaves to garnish
150g (5 oz) chèvre goat's cheese, in a roll	

Preheat the grill to its highest setting.

1 Mix together the oil and garlic in a small ramekin or bowl.

2 Thinly slice the baguette, and brush both sides with the garlic-flavoured olive oil. Place the bread on a small baking sheet which will fit under the grill, or line the grill pan with foil.

3 To cook the crostini, toast under the grill for about 2–3 minutes each side until pale golden brown and crisp. Watch them carefully. Cool on a wire rack.

4 Mash the chèvre (use the rind as well) with a little cream. Spread on to the cold crostini, keeping a little back. Drain and dry about 15 peppers, coarsely chop and arrange on the cheese. Dot the peppers with an additional piece of cheese.

5 Heat the crostini for about 5 minutes under the preheated hot grill. Garnish each crostini with a basil leaf.

cook now, eat later

TO PREPARE AND COOK AHEAD Prepare to step 4 up to 8 hours ahead. Cover with clingfilm and keep in the fridge until ready to cook. Flash under a hot grill for 5 minutes when guests arrive.

TO FREEZE The crostini bases can be made up to 2 months ahead and frozen. Leave at room temperature until defrosted.

TO COOK IN THE AGA To cook the crostini bases, bake on a solid baking sheet on the floor of the Roasting Oven for about 5–6 minutes until pale golden, turning half-way through the cooking time. Spread the cold crostini with the cheese and peppers and reheat on the second set of runners in the Roasting Oven for about 5 minutes until warm right through.

INDEX